C210406667

CW00308299

1 1 JUL 2015		
0 1 AUG 2015		

D&P/4261/4.12

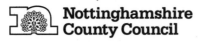

Nottinghamshire County Council

Please return / renew by the last date shown.

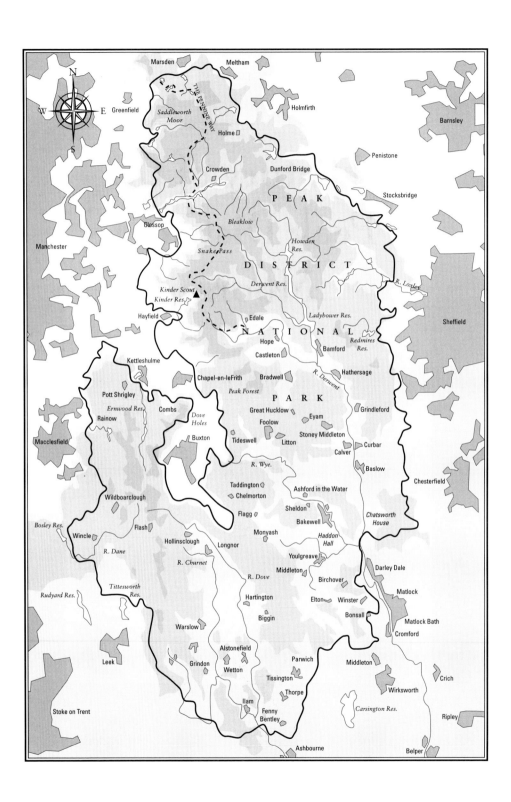

A History of the Peak District Moors

David Hey

Pen & Sword
LOCAL

First published in Great Britain in 2014 by
Pen & Sword Local
an imprint of
Pen & Sword Books Ltd
47 Church Street
Barnsley
South Yorkshire
S70 2AS

Copyright © David Hey 2014

ISBN 978 1 78346 281 0

A CIP catalogue record for this book is available from the British
Library

Typeset in Ehrhardt by
Mac Style, Bridlington, East Yorkshire
Printed and bound in the UK by CPI Group (UK) Ltd, Croydon,
CRO 4YY

Pen & Sword Books Ltd incorporates the imprints of Pen & Sword
Archaeology, Atlas, Aviation, Battleground, Discovery, Family History,
History, Maritime, Military, Naval, Politics, Railways, Select,
Social History, Transport, True Crime, and Claymore Press,
Frontline Books, Leo Cooper, Praetorian Press, Remember When,
Seaforth Publishing and Wharncliffe.

For a complete list of Pen & Sword titles please contact
PEN & SWORD BOOKS LIMITED
47 Church Street, Barnsley, South Yorkshire, S70 2AS, England
E-mail: enquiries@pen-and-sword.co.uk
Website: www.pen-and-sword.co.uk

Contents

Preface

I have lived on the edge of the Peak District for most of my life and walking across the moors remains my chief recreation. I spent my childhood in the hamlet of Catshaw and my youth 2 or 3 miles further down the Upper Don Valley at Penistone. As a student I got to know the Staffordshire Moorlands and as a young teacher the moors around Holmfirth. For the past forty years I've lived at Dronfield Woodhouse, ten minutes away from Longshaw. I'm a past president of the South Yorkshire and North-East Derbyshire Area of the Ramblers' Association and I'm a local historian who has spent much of his professional life researching the history of this area in the national and local archives. I've been very fortunate in having had the opportunity to combine my job with my hobby. This book is aimed in particular at the sort of people who realise that the enjoyment of a good walk in beautiful surroundings is enhanced by a knowledge of how that environment has come to be what it is today.

The book covers all periods of time from prehistory to the present. A typical moorland walk might take in the standing stones of a prehistoric stone circle, a medieval boundary marker, a guide stoop dated 1709, the straight walls of nineteenth-century enclosure, a row of Victorian grouse butts, a long line of flagstones brought in by helicopter, and very much more besides. Some of this physical evidence remains puzzling, but most of it can be explained by assiduous research in local record offices. I have not referenced the documents, as that would have made the book twice as long, but the bibliography provides leads to where the information may be found. For instance, I have written a fully referenced article, 'Kinder Scout and the Legend of the Mass Trespass' in *The Agricultural History Review*, vol. 59, part II (2011), pp. 199–216. I would be pleased to respond to enquiries as to where particular documentary evidence may be seen.

The friends who have helped me over the years are far too numerous to list, but the bibliography gives an indication of publications I have found particularly rewarding. Local history is a joint venture where we can all make a contribution. The pleasure derived from it is greatly enhanced by what Bert Ward, the great pioneer of rambling in the Peak District, called 'the trinity of legs, eyes and mind'.

David Hey
April 2013

For Richard, Dan and Matt, moorland ramblers

Chapter 1

Introduction: The Longshaw Estate

The meaning of 'moor'

When we speak of moors we may have two very different types of landscape in mind. Most of us immediately think of the barren uplands of the Pennines and the North York Moors, or perhaps of the similar rugged terrain of Bodmin Moor, Dartmoor and Exmoor in the south-west. But for others the word is associated with low-lying, wet districts such as the Old Moor at Wombwell (now a RSPB sanctuary) or the peat moors near Hatfield and Thorne to the east of Doncaster.

In the sixteenth century, John Leland, King Henry VIII's topographer, described the Isle of Axholme, just across the border from Thorne in Lincolnshire, as 'fenny, morische, and full of carrs'. The Anglo-Saxons, who came from lowland countries beyond the North Sea, seem to have applied their word *mor* particularly to areas such as these. Oliver Rackham tells us that *mor* occurs 174 times in Anglo-Saxon charters and that the context 'always demands the fen or bog sense', as indeed do many place-names containing *mor* from that time. Yet the Anglo-Saxons also used *mor* to translate the Latin *mons*, meaning 'mountain', and *moor* in the upland sense also appeared in their place-names. Perhaps two separate words came to have the same form, or perhaps the sense of boggy, barren land was applied to the hills once the Anglo-Saxons got that far inland. But if so, the meaning of the word must have changed over the centuries for it was eventually used to include dry heath and grass. It is now applied generally to any uncultivated parts of the Pennines and other highland areas.

Upland moors form a very distinctive British landscape; about 80 per cent of the world's heather moorland is found in the British Isles. But the Peak District moors once looked very different from what they do now. It is hard for us to imagine that in early prehistoric times they were quite well-wooded. Today's moors are not just the remnants of a 'natural' landscape, formed by the underlying geology, soils and vegetation, as many people suppose, for they have been influenced by thousands of years of human activity. It is often the case, for instance, that a large patch of grassland, devoid of heather, is the result not of natural forces but of the long-term digging of peat for domestic fires in the nearby farms and cottages or as fuel for local industries. And though we tend to speak of 'the moors' as if they are all the same, each one has its own individual character and a name that is usually taken from the nearest settlement, as with Abney Moor and Eyam Moor or Langsett Moors and Midhope Moors. Collectively, they owe much of their present appearance to their widespread use for grouse-shooting after they had been enclosed within drystone walls in the late eighteenth and early nineteenth centuries.

Longshaw over the centuries

The National Trust's estate at Longshaw, just over 7 miles south-west of the centre of Sheffield, provides some of the most accessible moorland and woodland for ramblers to enjoy. It lies just inside Derbyshire and adjoins the city boundary for a couple of miles at about 1,000 feet above sea level. Young and old people alike find plenty of interest within the estate's 5-mile circumference or as the start of a longer walk up on to the surrounding ridges. Many a child who came for a paddle in Burbage Brook and an ice-cream afterwards learned to love moorland scenery at an early age. A visit here is a perfect introduction to the Dark Peak, as we now call the gritstone moorlands. This distinguishes them from the limestone plateau and deep gorges of the White Peak. Longshaw illustrates every aspect of the long and changing history of this distinctive scenery, from the first prehistoric settlers to the present day.

The contribution of prehistoric people to the creation of the view looking north from the Visitors' Centre at Longshaw Lodge is not immediately apparent, yet finds of scattered flints show that hunter-gatherers were here in the Mesolithic era, the technical name for the Middle Stone Age. Our eyes are first attracted to the natural rocky profile of Higger Tor, the 'higher tor' on the skyline. 'Tor' is a term that most people associate with Devon, but it has been used in Derbyshire too since at least the Middle Ages and probably much earlier. Mam Tor, the 'breast-shaped hill' towering above the western end of Hope Valley, is the one that everyone knows, but many other examples can be found. Our view from Longshaw takes in Owler Tor below the Surprise View car park and Over Owler Tor near Mother Cap stone on the skyline beyond. Owler is a dialect word for an alder tree, which is found in local place-names such as Owler Bar and Owlerton. Just below Higger Tor another prominent escarpment has the intriguing name of Carl Wark, 'the work of the karls or churls', Viking and Anglo-Saxon words for the better-off peasants. The name must have arisen in the Middle Ages to suggest something that was created long ago. From Longshaw Lodge we see it as a natural rocky plateau with steep sides, but the approach from Higger Tor is much easier and so on the northern side a forbidding, massive wall of sturdy boulders was erected by herculean labour. The wall looks almost modern but is probably 2,000–3,000 years old. Just beyond it, on the western side, an entrance that was fashioned from the rocks can still be used to gain access to the summit.

Carl Wark has traditionally been interpreted as an Iron Age hill fort, but the truth of the matter is that we do not really know what its purpose was. Certainly in the Middle Ages local people regarded it as an old fort, for they named the stream below it the Burbage Brook, 'the stream near the fortification'. The brook had acquired this name by the early thirteenth century when it was recorded in a Latin document as *Aque de Burbache*, 'Burbage water'. But though the massive wall looks defensive, the summit is strewn with boulders and no signs of dwellings or any other prehistoric

This impressive wall on the northern side of Carl Wark dates from the late Bronze Age or the Iron Age.

features have been detected there. It looks a singularly unattractive place to have lived. Perhaps, then, it was not a fort but a communal gathering place at certain times of the year, similar in purpose to that on Gardom's Edge, which was once thought to have a Neolithic or New Stone Age origin but has now been placed in the late Bronze Age. At the moment we simply do not know the purpose of Carl Wark, but the consensus is that it dates from somewhere in the first millennium BC, when the Bronze Age merged into the Iron Age.

The other evidence of prehistoric activity around Longshaw is far less obvious but has been revealed by the careful fieldwork of archaeologists, particularly those working for the Peak District National Park Authority at Bakewell. Between Carl Wark and Toad's Mouth rock the low mounds of numerous cairns are dotted around the landscape. Some of these mark burial sites but others are simply piles of stones that have been cleared to create small fields; they are hard to distinguish without systematic excavation. Both types date from the Bronze Age, before the moors had acquired their present appearance with the encroachment of peat. They form part of an impressive collection of similar sites that extend southwards towards Chatsworth on the moors to the east of the River Derwent. We shall see that these Eastern Moors form one of the best-preserved Bronze Age landscapes in England. A casual walker will miss these cairns above Toad's Mouth, but the careful observer will develop an eye for them and will spot more in other parts of the Longshaw Estate. It will soon become clear that the development of this attractive landscape has been influenced by human activities over thousands of years.

The medieval evidence is equally compelling. 'Shaw' is a common minor place-name for a strip or wedge of woodland, but where this particular long strip was located cannot now be identified. Longshaw occupied the eastern edge of the parish of Hathersage, the Burbage Brook acting in part as the boundary with the chapelry of Dore within the parish of Dronfield. It seems to have been used as a common pasture, particularly by the inhabitants of the hamlet of Highlow, which lies on the other side of the River Derwent but still within the parish of Hathersage. The earliest documentary record that has come to light is a letter of 1722 to William Archer of London (formerly William Eyre of Highlow Hall, who had changed his name upon an inheritance), which says about Longshaw: 'your grandfather kept a great flock of sheep there every summer'. At the end of the eighteenth century the Highlow farmers still enjoyed common rights of pasture in this border zone. It seems entirely appropriate that the large Longshaw Meadow that is now the venue for the annual September sheep-dog trials should have a long history as part of an ancient sheepwalk. The farmers of the neighbouring parishes too grazed their sheep and cattle on the moors around Longshaw and they sometimes got involved in arguments as to where their boundaries lay. A striking reminder of the importance attached to boundary markers is provided by the Wooden Pole on the skyline behind Longshaw Lodge. The pole has been replaced from time to time, but the stone base into which it is set is inscribed 'T1778', signifying the date when the inhabitants of Totley made a perambulation of their boundaries, in this case with the parish of Hathersage. Less obvious now are the initials of Thomas Willoughby, the Lord of Totley at that time, which were also carved into the stone. Totley village lies out of sight 3 miles away to the east, so we get an immediate sense of the great extent of the common pastures and wastes that were available to its householders and cottagers.

The Longshaw Estate is particularly suited to the grazing of sheep, but when the national population rose to unprecedented levels in the twelfth and thirteenth centuries, a somewhat desperate attempt was made to cultivate

The foundations of a medieval longhouse at Lawrence Field above Padley Gorge are a remarkable survival. The building would have been shared by a farming family at the top of the slope (front) and their cattle below, beyond a cross-passage entry.

part of this land and to grow crops there for the first time since the Bronze Age. Perhaps these efforts were supervised by the lord of the manor of Padley or his steward, for they took place high above Padley Gorge. The best evidence can be found in the area known as Lawrence Field, on the shelf between the gorge and Owler Tor, where a large oval enclosure, about 300 metres long and 200 metres wide, was protected by an outer ditch and upright stones were erected on a small bank, which can be traced (with some difficulty) amongst the heather. The boundaries that divided this enclosure into strips, which were presumably shared by the farmers who had cleared the land in an arduous, co-operative enterprise, are now difficult to find. We can only marvel at the labour involved in removing the boulders and placing some of them in an encircling wall before oats could be sown on this bleak, unpromising site, which has long since reverted to heather moorland. The sections of the wall that remain are best seen on the southern side of the enclosure, where they run parallel to the birch wood at the top of the gorge.

Most remarkable of all are the stone foundations of a contemporary farmhouse on the south-eastern side of the enclosure where the land begins its steep descent into the gorge at the top of Padley Wood. It was built in the typical style of a medieval longhouse to provide domestic accommodation at the top end and a cattle byre down the slope. The foundations of a smaller outbuilding can be seen nearby. Potsherds that have been unearthed at the longhouse site date from about the twelfth century.

Meanwhile, a similar clearance scheme was underway on the other side of Padley Gorge in the area now marked on Ordnance Survey maps as Sheffield Plantation. Some of the earthworks there indicate that prehistoric families once farmed this land; the medieval evidence consists of lines of tumbled-down field walls. This enterprise may not have lasted long, for when the Black Death of 1348–49 reduced the national population by at least a third, and perhaps by a half, the demand for land slackened and sites such as these, at over 900 feet above sea level on thin, unproductive soils, were soon abandoned. On Dartmoor, we can see that this happened at the deserted hamlet of Hound Tor, which has been fully excavated.

Farming was not the only activity in the Longshaw district during the Middle Ages. There are signs of quarrying, especially for millstones, all around us. The old name for Padley Gorge was Yarncliff, 'the eagle cliff', so these noble birds of prey must once have built their nests in the upper reaches of the ancient coppice woods that rise steeply on either side of the stream as it rushes down towards Grindleford. An account of millstone-hewing in

1466 at *Ernclyfe* is preserved in the form of some small cashbooks that were kept by Ralph Eyre of Offerton. Eyre employed a group of eight hewers on a piece-rate basis under the supervision of an overseer and a chapman who saw to their distribution. One of the workers had the appropriate name of Jankyn Stonehewer, a surname that survives in small numbers to this day, particularly on the western side of the Peak District.

The hewers were paid to produce pairs of finished millstones of 15 or 16 hands in diameter, a hand being a precise measurement of 4 inches. These medieval accounts tally with the eleven millstones of 60 inches diameter and the four larger stones of 64 inches diameter that Helen Egan found, amongst others of different sizes, in her survey of Yarncliff Wood, so it is possible that some of these unfinished stones were abandoned upon the discovery of flaws over five centuries ago; the smaller stones were used as the uppermost of each pair in milling flour. The hewing of millstones was anciently a seasonal occupation. Eyre's accounts for 1466 note that William Wethyngton had agreed to work at Yarncliff until Martinmas (11 November) and that John Barker had contracted to make three pairs of millstones by that date. Finished pairs were supplied to mills as far away as Loughborough, some 45 miles distant.

Abandoned millstones can also be found in large numbers above the Surprise View car park near Mother Cap stone; on Reeve's Edge, high above the Burbage Brook; and in a quarry at the top of Padley Gorge that was approached by a long, well-structured track, surrounded by huge piles of debris. But these stones were not used for corn milling. Instead they were intended for pulping wood at paper mills, for grinding paint, or for making animal feed stock. Most of the surviving millstones on the neighbouring moors were left there because buyers could no longer be found for them; the latest ones date from the 1920s and 1930s. The quarries were also used for making troughs, lintels and gateposts, some of which lie abandoned in an unfinished and flawed condition. The natural rugged character of the gritstone edges of the local moors was greatly enhanced by all this industrial activity. The spectacular escarpment that hides the Surprise View has been known as Millstone Edge since at least 1625. Its alternative name of Booth Edge was taken from the medieval cattle-rearing farm that lay below it.

The millstone industry has also left a series of holloways, or hollowgates, that were dug out to make a relatively smooth surface for the transport of stones from the quarries to the highways. Looking across Longshaw Meadow and the Burbage Brook we see the deepest and most spectacular of

This small quarry or 'delph' at the top of Padley Gorge was abandoned in the first half of the twentieth century. Millstones had been hewn in this gorge for about 500 years.

Moving newly finished millstones from the quarry face to the highways was a tricky business, fraught with the danger of damaging the stones. Some quarry owners paid for the digging of holloways to create a relatively smooth incline so that horses could pull the stones on sledges. This one from Millstone Edge towards Longshaw is thought to date from the late seventeenth century when John Rotherham of Dronfield leased the quarry.

these artificial holloways, descending from Millstone Edge. It was probably dug out late in the seventeenth century, when John Rotherham of Dronfield leased the quarry from the Duke of Norfolk, in order to ease the movement of millstones on horse-drawn sledges. The old fording stones are still in place in the Burbage Brook by the present foot bridge. Then the holloways divide, one group heading towards Fox House and the other climbing into Sheffield Plantation before heading across the Big Moor towards the inland port of Bawtry. At the time, Peak District millstones were the most famous in England for the grinding of oats and other inferior grains, but French and German stones were preferred for wheat.

Millstone hewing was not the only industry on the Peak District moors. In the Middle Ages many a windy escarpment was used for smelting lead in primitive hearths known as boles. One of these gave its name to Bole Hill, high above Padley Gorge. The woods in the gorge were coppiced well into Victoria's reign, and the huge quarry that was worked at Bole Hill in the

Even the thin soils of Padley Gorge once supported coppiced woodland, consisting mainly of sessile oaks and birch, but with alder by the swiftly descending brook and scattered hollies and rowans. These gnarled and twisted oaks spring from stools that were last coppiced in mid-Victorian times.

early years of the twentieth century was the source of the building stones for the Howden and Derwent dams, the large reservoirs that provide drinking water for many parts of the Midlands. After the removal of the debris of the millstone makers and the construction of workshops, sheds, railways and loading bays, quarrying began in earnest. Some 350–450 men were employed there during a 7½-year period when over 1.2 million tons of stones were sent to the Upper Derwent Valley. For ten hours every working day a hydraulic ram pumped 12,000 gallons of water from a stream below.

The quarry faces at Bole Hill and Millstone Edge and the cast-offs that litter the ground below the escarpment still bear the shot holes and channels by which stones were removed by blasts of gunpowder. Travelling cranes, powered by steam, raised the newly cut stones into trucks, which were then moved by rail to the top of a steep incline that descended to the railway at Grindleford. This incline was worked by cables connected to a self-winding drum, the weight of each full truck on the descent pulling an empty truck back up.

The incline is now overgrown but can still be followed, with difficulty, down into the valley. The former quarry is eerily silent and colonised by birch trees. Its rock faces now pose a series of interesting challenges to young climbers.

Roads

Motorists who drive through the Longshaw Estate follow the lines of eighteenth- and nineteenth-century turnpike roads, some of which were improvements of much more ancient highways. The old routes that were closed to the public after the Duke of Rutland built Longshaw Lodge are now difficult to follow. A mid-eighteenth-century packhorse bridge, which spans Burbage Brook below Carl Wark, was built to serve travellers on the

Packhorse bridges date from the seventeenth or eighteenth century, when they often replaced wooden structures. Many were demolished when turnpike trusts provided wider bridges to take wheeled vehicles, but some survive across the upper reaches of moorland streams. This one crossed the Burbage Brook below Carl Wark on the bridleway from Dore to Hathersage. It has no parapets.

Dore to Hathersage bridleway who came over Reeve's Edge and aimed for the skyline at Winyards Nick. Two guide stoops from the same era mark other routes through the estate. Stoop is a North Country word, derived from the language of the Vikings, for a post.

There is a tall one that can be seen about 100 yards to the north of the gateposts that marks the drive that leads from Longshaw Lodge towards the Grouse Inn. It is among the sturdiest of the many stoops that the Derbyshire

The Derbyshire JPs first ordered the construction of guide stoops across lonely moors in 1709. This one uses phonetic spelling in the local dialect to point the way to Sheffield. Some stoops were inscribed with pointing hands, but the implicit method here is to face the inscription then turn to the right.

justices of the peace ordered to be erected in 1709 to guide travellers across the moors and other lonely places.

Because of changes to the landscape when conifers were planted in the nineteenth century, it is now hard to believe that this stoop once stood at an important crossroads. But the inscriptions on its four sides point the ways to the nearest market towns. The destinations are indicated in phonetic spellings that reflect the broad speech of the times: 'To Tidswel, To Chasterfild, To Shafild 1709', and best of all, 'To Hatharsich And So To Chapil in Lee Frith'. Perhaps Chapel-en-le-Frith was added when the masons realised that Hathersage was not a market town.

We can work out the directions that were taken from the stoop. Tideswell was reached via Grindleford Bridge, the Sir William Hill, and the ridgeway to Great Hucklow. Chesterfield was approached via the Wooden Pole and a route across the Big Moor. Travellers heading for Sheffield crossed Houndkirk Moor, and those going in the opposite direction to Hathersage, perhaps used the millstone road to the Surprise View.

The other guide stoop in Longshaw Park is not in its original position. It now stands just inside the entrance gate on the approach to the lodge from the road leading from Fox House to Grindleford. It was recovered by National Trust staff in the late 1960s and placed there because its exact former site was not known. But it was aligned incorrectly, for the old practice was to face the inscription and then turn to the right. Many other old stoops have pointing fingers that confirm this custom. This small stoop is one of several that were erected in 1737, when the Derbyshire JPs decided that the original provision in 1709 was insufficient to meet the needs of travellers through the Peak District. On one side it is inscribed 'Hope Rode 1737', on its other faces 'Sheiffeild Rode, Dronfield Rode, Tidswal Rode', so it marked the same route system as the earlier stoop at the other side of the lodge. As a market had been established in Hope in 1715, the long inscription to Hathersage and Chapel-en-le-Frith on the 1709 stoop was no longer needed.

By the mid-eighteenth century the movement to upgrade the major highways into turnpike roads where tolls were paid by travellers was well underway. The first one across Longshaw was the Sheffield to Tideswell and Buxton turnpike road of 1758, which came over Houndkirk Moor from Ringinglow. The character of an old moorland highway before modern road surfaces were introduced is well-preserved here, for in 1812 this route was largely replaced by the present road from Sheffield via Hunter's Bar, Banner Cross and Whirlow to Fox House. A milestone near Thieves Bridge is inscribed 'Tideswell 10, Buxton 17' on one side and 'Sheffield 6' on the other. The road reached Longshaw by descending to Fox House, which was named after its owner, a Mr Fox of Callow Bank. This inn was completely rebuilt by the Duke of Rutland about 1830 in the same mock-Jacobean style as his new lodge.

The continuation of the turnpike road through Longshaw Meadow was blocked off and the present complicated system of road turnings was created, so that the route down to Grindleford was set further back from the ducal view from his lodge. The former route through the meadow is indicated by another turnpike milestone that is shaped in the same style as the one on Houndkirk Moor and which marks 8 miles from Sheffield on one side and 8 miles from Tideswell and 15 miles from Buxton on the other.

Beyond Granby Wood, the original line of the turnpike road can be picked up again as it descends towards the junction with the present road at Yarncliff Cottage. This old route is now a pleasant grassy track, but it is supported firmly by a strong embankment on the north-western side. It must have been a steep climb for horse-drawn coaches coming the other way up the hill from Grindleford.

Meanwhile, in 1781 another old route out of Sheffield and north-east Derbyshire had been turnpiked. This came via Greenhill, Bradway, Holmesfield and Owler Bar. Near the Wooden Pole one branch turned left down the hill to Calver and Stoney Middleton, while the other continued to Fox House, Toad's Mouth and along the present route to Hathersage. The original descent from near the Wooden Pole to Fox House followed what is now a grassy track below the pole down to Longshaw Lodge, but by Victorian times this had become a private drive that took the guests at the lodge on to the moors. Near Toad's Mouth rock, a cast-iron turnpike milestone is inscribed 'Hathersage 2, Castleton 8, Chapel-en-le-Frith 14' on one side and 'Sheffield 8' on the other. The cutting at Millstone Edge, which produces the Surprise View, was made in 1826.

The enclosure of the commons and wastes

In the opening decades of the nineteenth century the moors around Longshaw were divided into private ownership and common rights, such as the grazing of livestock and the digging of peat for fuel, were extinguished. Throughout England and Wales upland commons and wastes were enclosed by numerous private Acts of Parliament. These Acts dealt with individual parishes or their sub-divisions, the townships, and if the owners of about seventy-five to eighty per cent of the land (in terms of rateable value) agreed to enclose they were able to impose their will on the other owners.

Commissioners and surveyors were employed to divide the commons into 'allotments' in lieu of the common rights that had been attached to each farm. The largest landowners, therefore, got the biggest shares and the lord of the manor was compensated further for his loss of other rights. In the huge parishes that straddled the Pennines, lords opted to receive large stretches of the 'wastes', tracts of little value that could be converted into grouse moors. For example, when the 2,650 acres of Holmesfield township were enclosed between 1816 and 1820, the Duke of Rutland was awarded 1,998 acres of the least productive land. By such means, and by purchases, the duke gradually acquired a huge grouse moor that also included former commons and wastes within the parishes and townships of Barlow, Baslow, Brampton, Hathersage, Dore and Totley. Longshaw was transformed from a sheepwalk into the headquarters of the largest grouse-shooting estate in the Peak District.

As we do not have access to the duke's archives, we are unable to date the various sequences of the building of Longshaw Lodge, but the original

The Duke of Rutland built Longshaw Lodge in the years around 1830 to accommodate his guests, especially in the grouse-shooting season. The Ice House, which was used to freeze game and other food, is well-hidden in a deep underground chamber to the rear of the lodge.

'shooting box' may have been erected a few years before it was mentioned in William White's *Directory* of 1833. The duke seems to have acquired this portion of the Hathersage moors before the publication of the award in 1830, when a building named Longshaw was marked on the accompanying map where the lodge now stands. The lodge, which was erected for house guests during the shooting season, was designed in a mock-Jacobean style to give it a false sense of antiquity, with gables, mullioned windows with emphatic mouldings, and a four-storey battlemented tower to the rear. A chapel, servants' quarters and extensive stables were also provided.

The gamekeepers who were employed to rear the grouse were housed in cottages that were sometimes built in the same Jacobean style. One stands at the entrance to the drive, but those on Ramshaw and Burbage moors have been demolished. The most dramatic are two identical cottages. White Edge Lodge, just below the escarpment of that name, which The National Trust has converted into a holiday home; and Thickwood Lodge on the left-hand side of the road that descends from Owler Bar to Totley. As we have noted, Fox House Inn was also rebuilt in an imitation of the Jacobean style and the turnpike road was pushed back beyond the meadow in front of the lodge to keep unwanted travellers at bay. A large fishpond was created to improve the view and to provide fare for the guests, and in the days before refrigeration, fish and meat were kept frozen with ice from the ice house that can still be seen, dug deep into the earth to the rear of the lodge.

Upon the enclosure of the Hathersage commons and wastes, some of the new 'allotments' were purchased by Charles Brookfield, a Sheffield solicitor of Paradise Square, on behalf of himself and several friends. They had all formed the Sheffield Planting Company on 28 August 1823 with a capital stock of £5,750 to fence and drain the moorland in the western part of Longshaw and to plant timber. Their property – which is still marked as Sheffield Plantation on Ordnance Survey maps – was intersected by the original turnpike road from Sheffield to Buxton and divided into two parts, amounting to 180 acres. The twenty-one shareholders were Sheffield gentlemen and businessmen including Josiah and William Fairbank, the surveyors. This venture has left a permanent imprint on the landscape, where conifers grow on raised banks divided by drainage ditches. The partners also kept an eye open for other projects that might make money.

In December 1835 Christopher Green Broomhead of Fulwood was asked to see if the stone in the plantation (adjoining the Grindleford Bridge Road) was suitable for making millstones, and a ten-year lease at a yearly rent of twenty-five guineas was arranged. In 1844 a cottage for the woodman was built in the plantation. Was this, one wonders, the one that bears the name Yarncliff Cottage and which, in later times at least, was a keeper's cottage on the duke's estate?

The company's initial relationship with its aristocratic neighbour at the shooting lodge was not an easy one. A minute book records that, at a meeting held on 5 December 1832, it was resolved that 'the Duke of Rutland, having by his agent applied to the company for the privilege of making a drive or road through the plantation from Longshaw to the Grindleford Bridge Road, the meeting did not think it expedient to grant his grace such a privilege'. At another meeting, held at Fox House on 24 May 1833, Josiah Fairbank was requested 'to view the diversion of water, made by the duke, and to prepare a plan of the same and report to the next meeting'. This was held on 12 July, when the surveyor reported that the diversion had been made to supply the duke's fish pond, that it was injurious to the plantation, and that it ought not to have been made without the company's consent. The duke's agent agreed to restore the water to its former channels.

In October 1833 instructions were given to carry the drive through the plantation up to Froggatt Edge Road and to provide stone posts for a good substantial gate for the entrance there. This must be the drive that turns off the highway above the Grouse Inn and continues all the way to Longshaw Lodge, through the gateposts that mark the boundary between the estates of the company and the duke. The company continued to assert its independence in the following decade. At a general meeting of shareholders held in Sheffield on 5 December 1842 it was resolved that no one be allowed to shoot or otherwise destroy game within the plantation bounds, and in July 1844 it was decided that 'the privilege, which had been temporarily allowed to the duke, of a footpath through the plantation from Longshaw to Yarncliff be discontinued'. But in the end enthusiasm for the timber enterprise waned and at a special meeting held in Sheffield on 9 October 1854 the members considered an offer by the duke's agent either to lease shooting rights within the plantation or to buy the estate.

The plantation was eventually sold to the duke for £3,300 and the company was dissolved in 1856. The Duke of Rutland now possessed the whole of Longshaw. Between 1868 and 1871 he planted more conifers beyond the fishpond in Granby Wood, which was named after his eldest son, the Marquis of Granby.

The hey-day of grouse-shooting was in the late Victorian and Edwardian periods. The record annual 'bag' on the moorland estate that was centred on Longshaw was the 3,633 brace of grouse that were shot in 1893. During

About the same time as he built Longshaw Lodge, the Duke of Rutland constructed gamekeepers' cottages in the same Jacobean style. This one on the skyline below White Edge has now been turned into holiday accommodation by The National Trust.

the First World War grouse-shooting was abandoned and Longshaw Lodge was used as an auxiliary hospital. After the war, game birds were killed on an enormous scale once again; in 1921, for instance, the 'bag' on this estate was 3,002 brace of grouse, fifty-three brace of pheasants, ten brace of partridges, and some hares and rabbits.

One unusual effect on the moorland landscape was the creation of five fields enclosed by sturdy drystone walls. These fields are now mostly barren and overgrown with heather, but one that still catches the eye to the north of Winyards Nick is a 21-acre enclosure, with a sheepfold in one corner to provide shelter in severe weather. These fields were set aside for the growing of black oats in order to feed the grouse and perhaps to provide crops of winter hay for sheep. It was the custom for thousands of sheep from bleaker parts of north Derbyshire to be pastured on the moors around Longshaw during the winter months, but the duke stopped this practice in 1924 so that his grouse would have enough heather to feed on. By then, however, the shooting of grouse on the Longshaw estate was about to end.

The right to roam and the sale of the Longshaw Estate

The enclosure of the commons and wastes and the creation of grouse moors meant the loss of public access. Hostile gamekeepers and weekend 'watchers' were employed by the Duke of Rutland and other landowners to prevent people from walking across some former rights of way. In 1926 the duke even ordered his tenants at Higger Lodge, high on Burbage Moor, to stop making tea for ramblers. In a series of '*Sheffield Telegraph*' *Rambles*, published in 1913, Chas H. Chandler wrote that Carl Wark:

> is more effectually protected now than ever it was in the days of the Ancient Britons. Every path leading to it displays a 'Trespassers will be prosecuted' notice … The fort and the Tor are now preserved for grouse and rabbits, which are very plentiful in that valley of desolation where men rarely walk.

Following a campaign by the writer John Derry, and others in the *Sheffield Independent*, in 1909, the duke's agent provided G.H.B. Ward, the founder of the Sheffield Clarion Ramblers, with a written promise to allow parties of not more than six persons at a time to walk along Froggatt Edge. But in

Linda Raby, the granddaughter of G. H. B. Ward, at the opening of the Moorland Dicovery Centre's landscape garden at Longshaw in 2009, with Mike Innerdale (The National Trust's general manager for the Peak District) and the author (representing The Ramblers' Association).

1924 the duke reneged on this undertaking and ordered his gamekeepers to turn walkers away. At about the same time, some of the entrances to the Longshaw 'drives' were walled up.

As we shall see in Chapter 7, in those years Ward was the leading agitator for 'the right to roam' in the Peak District. He was unafraid of wandering over the moors, especially where he was convinced that an old bridleway or footpath had been closed illegally. He was not only a most active and vociferous rambler but also a pioneering historian of the local landscape. He sought out features such as sunken tracks, packhorse bridges, guide stoops and medieval boundary stones on the moors, he noted the memories of local farmers and their use of minor place-names, and he spent hours of study in the archives section of Sheffield Reference Library researching historical documents and maps that would explain his discoveries on the ground. In the *Sheffield Clarion Ramblers Handbook* for 1927–28 he published a long account of his findings about the Big Moor at the core of the Longshaw moorland estate. It is entirely appropriate that in 2009 a large part of a generous legacy, which he left upon the death of his daughter, was spent on the creation of a garden at the Moorland Discovery Centre at Longshaw, which now bears the name of Ward's Croft.

The first major breakthrough in the establishment of a right to roam on the Peak District moors came in 1927 when the Duke of Rutland was forced to sell the Longshaw Estate, and much other property in north Derbyshire, in order to pay death duties. The ducal family had owned this estate for about a hundred years, but like many other aristocrats were now feeling the pinch because of these duties and declining agricultural rents. The 11,533 acres of the Longshaw Estate and the 747 acres of the park were advertised for sale, including 9,633 acres of grouse moorland and additional sporting rights over 2,200 acres of adjacent farmland. The 'Famous Sporting Moors, well heathered and easily reached by good motoring roads' formed a compact estate, listed separately as Houndkirk & Burbage Moors (2,407 acres), Big Moor (3,111), Totley Moor (1,118), Clod Hall Moor (866), Leash Fen Moor (681), Blacka Moor (448), Ramsley Moor (638) and Eaglestone Flat Moor (394), which in good years had produced together over 8,000 brace of grouse. It was claimed that the moors ranked among the best and most accessible in England and that 'since the War they have been regularly and judiciously burned, and are now in good condition, and considerable sums have been spent over an extended period on drainage with excellent results'. The sale also included keepers' lodges, the Fox House, Peacock and Chequers pubs, several small farms, valuable quarries and woodlands.

To the delight of local ramblers, the 747-acre Longshaw Park was treated separately in the sale. A Longshaw Committee was immediately formed to raise funds to purchase the park and to hand it over to The National Trust. In the words of G.H.B. Ward, it was 'in effect, a ramblers' committee; for the names of [its members] bring to mind the doers of many doughty deeds and walks, and one is proud to be associated with them'. They comprised several Sheffield industrialists and professionals, Ethel Gallimore of the CPRE (as secretary), a representative from the Peak District and Northern Counties Footpaths Preservation Society, and Phil Barnes and Stephen Morton, two young activists in the Sheffield Clarion Ramblers. By January 1928 over £9,000 of the £14,000 that was needed to complete the purchase had been raised. The handover of the deeds eventually took place before a large crowd that assembled in front of the lodge in 1933.

The 747 acres purchased by the original appeal stretched from just above the present Grouse Inn up to the Wooden Pole then down to Fox House, Toad's Mouth and The Surprise View, coming back along the ridge above the Bole Hill quarries and descending to Padley Gorge. In 1933 another 18 acres between Bole Hill and Padley Gorge, above Grindleford and Padley Chapel, were bought from income generated from the money raised by the appeal. Subsequently, a further 245½ acres, from the Surprise View to just above the Millstone Inn, then running alongside the railway line almost to Padley Chapel but excluding the disused Bole Hill quarries and incline from where stones had been transported to the Howden and Derwent dams, were added to the National Trust's property. Since then, the National Trust's Longshaw Estate has been extended to 1,600 acres to include the former Bole Hill quarries, together with woods in the south-west and woodland and fields associated with Greenwood Farm in the north-west.

The opening up of Longshaw was a major breakthrough for ramblers campaigning for the right to roam. It was here that the National Council of Ramblers' Federations, the forerunner of the Ramblers' Association, was formed in September 1931. Meanwhile, the moorland estate that had been organised from Longshaw Lodge had been divided between two local authorities. Chesterfield Rural District Council bought the Big Moor to safeguard the water supply from the reservoir that they had constructed in 1908, but they leased the shooting rights to William Wilson of Horsleygate Hall, Holmesfield, and continued to keep ramblers out. Burbage Moors, extending from Fox House, Toad's Mouth and Millstone Edge, together with the adjoining Houndkirk Moors, were purchased by Sheffield Corporation for £21,000 with the idea of constructing a reservoir in the Upper Burbage

During the Second World War military manoeuvres were held on the moors around the Burbage Valley. The stone seen here below Carl Wark was one of many prominent natural features that were used for target practice.

valley below Carl Wark, but mercifully this plan never came to fruition. Ramblers were allowed to roam over these moors and the Duke's Drive along this valley became a very popular walk from Longshaw Lodge or Fox House.

The campaign for access to the countryside was put on hold during the Second World War, when many of the local moors were used for military manoeuvres. The Packhorse Bridge and some of the prominent rocks below Carl Wark, for example, were used for target practice. After the war the army wished to keep a large stretch of moorland all the way from Totley on to the Big Moor as a military training ground, but thankfully the suggestion was rejected. Instead, in 1949 the National Parks and Access to the Countryside Act was passed and ten National Parks were created over the following decade, starting with the 555 square miles of the Peak District National Park in 1951. Huge stretches of the Peak District moorlands came under the control either of the Peak District National Park Authority or The National Trust. Longshaw Lodge was converted into the headquarters of the Trust's Longshaw and High Peak Estates and Padley Gorge was designated a Site of Special Scientific Interest as one of the most important attractions in Derbyshire for ornothologists in search of wood warblers, pied flycatchers, woodpeckers, wheatears, ring ouzels, jays, moorhen, dippers and kingfishers.

An estate that was once out of bounds to all but a few is now one of the most popular venues in the Peak District.

Chapter 2

The Early History of the Moors

The Stone Age

Botanists have used the technique of pollen analysis, correlated with radio-carbon dating, to show that at the end of the last Ice Age, about 10,000 years ago, the present moors of northern England looked very different from what they do now. As the ice retreated, the climate grew rapidly warmer and soon reached temperatures similar to those of today. Dwarf birch, juniper, thrift and buttercup covered the thin soils of the landscape. Then in the Mesolithic era (or Middle Stone Age) this mosaic was gradually replaced by wildwood, right up to the highest summits of the Pennines. Pollen samples from Cook's Study, at the head of the Holme Valley, 1,472 feet above sea level, indicate that the forest cover there consisted mainly of hazel, oak and alder with some birch and lime. Elsewhere in the Peak District, woodland in the valley bottoms was dominated by alder and possibly ash: the lower valley sides were covered by pine, oak and elm; and the upper valley sides and the lower summits were characterised by birch, hazel scrub and montane plant species. Within this broad picture, however, many exposed summits, cliffs, screes, areas of shallow soil, mires, springs and flushes had no tree cover.

Over a very long period of time, the soils in the upper areas became wet and acidic and so the vegetation gradually changed to hazel scrub, birch and willow. It seems likely that fire – whether natural or man-made – was also responsible for some of the long-term changes that produced the present moorland landscape. Peat began to form in basins with large catchments of water at the highest levels and as the rainfall increased blanket peat began to spread outwards in a process that started in later Mesolithic times, continued until the end of the Iron Age and, in some places, even later.

The Mesolithic era is defined loosely as the period from around 8000 BC to about 4500 BC, when the total population of Britain was only a few thousand. The people of that time lived in small groups in every type of countryside

The uninviting nature of much of the Kinder plateau is apparent from this view of exposed peat on the summit. Peat began to spread in the Stone Age, but the present landscape was thousands of years in the making.

but they left little mark on the landscape. Their distinctive tools and flakes, shaped from brown flints and black chert and secured to wooden or bone shafts with birch pitch for use as arrows, spears, harpoons, knives and edge-tools, have been found at what may have been their summer camps and perhaps a few more permanent settlements. Most of the flints and flakes that have been collected from the Peak District moors were preserved in sandy soils beneath a later covering of peat on the edges of gently eroded scarp slopes. Erosion has brought them to light. These uplands, rising from 1,200 to 1,600 feet, remained well-wooded, with patches of grassland or heath. A good example is the Harry Hut site on Chunal Moor, near Charlesworth, which seems to have been occupied from time-to-time between the sixth and fourth millennium BC.

Amateur collectors with a strong interest in prehistory have been particularly active in discovering evidence for Mesolithic activity on the Meltham and Marsden Moors, high above the Colne Valley. Sites include Warcock Hill, Cupwith Hill, Flint Hill, March Hill, Pule Hill and White Hill, all of which were close to passes that followed the contours of the land and probably used by hunting parties in the summer months. Several thousand pieces of flint, many of them shaped into tools, have been unearthed at Cupwith Hill, while four distinct workshop sites, which together produced over 6,000 flints, including 500 worked tools, have been identified at March Hill. Fewer sites have been discovered south-west of Meltham, but at West Nab, 1,641 feet above sea level, excavators found about 350 flints, including a number of cores, microliths, and worked and used pieces. Surface finds indicate other Mesolithic sites on the moors between Hepworth and Thurlstone and near Dunford Bridge, on elevated spurs and scarp edges close to abundant small streams and well-defined ridges. An excavated site at Cook's Study, situated on a gritstone-capped spur, produced numerous microliths, scrapers and gravers from the late Mesolithic era, when what is now bare moorland was still well-wooded and full of game.

Flint tools and weapons are almost the only evidence that Mesolithic people have left on the local moors. Many of their artefacts were made from wood, bone and skin and have not survived, and most of their dwellings must have been temporary or movable structures. A more permanent dwelling in which a family could have lived during the winter months was excavated in the early 1960s near the former Deepcar railway station in the valley of the Little Don, just off the moors, but this was an exceptional discovery that attracted widespread interest among prehistorians. The fauna of this era included red and roe deer, large wild cattle known as aurochs, wild boars, wolves and bears, and small mammals such as the fox, badger, wild cat, otter and beaver. Mesolithic people have been traditionally regarded as hunter-gatherers who followed a seasonal round, but prehistorians now place less emphasis on their hunting and fishing and more on their gathering of the abundant and varied plant foods that were available.

The New Stone Age or Neolithic era, dating from about 4500 to 2200 BC, saw the beginnings of settled farming, a practice that spread slowly across Europe from the Middle East. At Lismore Fields, at the start of the climb on to the moors above Buxton, an excavation in the mid-1980s led by Daryl Garton revealed the best-preserved evidence that has so far been discovered in Britain for well-built, rectangular, timber-framed buildings with central hearths that date back to the Early Neolithic period. Nothing survives above ground-level, but radiocarbon tests on material found in the postholes suggest a date of around 3500 BC. A few flints and flakes showed that Lismore Fields had been used in a different way even earlier, in the Mesolithic era. The site was occupied over an unusually long time, though continuous use cannot be proved. The Neolithic finds include pottery, a polished stone axe, flint and chert tools, and numerous charred cereal grains, hazelnuts and the fruit and seeds of crab apples. But the acidity of the clay soils has destroyed any bones of domesticated livestock or wild animals that might have been hunted. Several pits and nine small circular structures of unknown purpose and date were also found nearby. This is an archaeological site of national importance.

The Neolithic era was the time when trees began to be felled and the first major monuments in the form of henges and chambered barrows appeared on the limestone plateau of the White Peak. The present moorland landscapes around the White Peak were peripheral areas that were grazed on a smaller scale. Only a few Neolithic axes have been found there. The pollen record for the Eastern Moors shows that up to 3000 BC mixed oak forest, with a lot of alder in the wetter parts, had replaced earlier pine trees and that the forest cover was almost complete. Scatters of Neolithic potsherds and flint and chert tools have been found on the moors above the Upper Derwent Valley, but the earliest surviving earthworks are the burial mounds known as barrows, which were sited in prominent positions in the landscape during the later Neolithic period and beyond.

The Bronze Age

Human settlement on some of the present gritstone moors began in earnest in the Late Neolithic era and the Early Bronze Age. The moors to the east of the River Derwent, stretching from Bamford in the north to Beeley in the south, have provided some of England's most important archaeological evidence for this period. Further north and west, however, the higher parts of the Dark Peak are bleak and windswept, and only a small number of isolated round barrows have been found there; perhaps there is more to be found under the later layers of peat? Evidence of Bronze Age activities was preserved on suitable sites to the east of the river once the peat began to spread, even though the cultivation of crops was abandoned and the whole area was given over to grazing. The surviving features in the landscape are not easy to recognise when the heather is high, but controlled or accidental burning sometimes exposes the foundations of abandoned roundhouses within low, irregular field walls. More evident are the stone-clearance cairns, round barrows and small stone circles, which together demonstrate the extensive use of the landscape in this early period.

Most of the woods were cleared during the Bronze Age, when the climate was warmer and wetter than it is now. Pollen analysis on the Eastern Moors suggests that settlement there began about 1700 BC and reached its greatest extent 200 years later. Small family groups continued to farm this district until the beginnings of the Iron Age, after which the record is silent. When Stewart Ainsworth surveyed the Eastern Moors in 1993, he discovered the foundations of round, timber-framed houses from the Bronze Age within 130 small, circular platforms. Although these were not all occupied at the same time, they suggest a sizeable local population before the peat had begun to spread. The soils that were cultivated in small plots consisted of light sands over the gritstones and heavier clays on the shales. They were sufficiently fertile for growing cereals as well as for grazing livestock, perhaps in rotation. Ancient field systems that were in use during the Late Neolithic era and the Bronze Age can still be traced in part on the Eastern Moors. Fields were enclosed in varying shapes and sizes by low stone walls and earthen banks, which veered around boulders that were too heavy to move, amidst small clearance cairns on patches of stony ground that were unsuitable for cultivation.

The best known site is that at Swine Sty, where a small group of farmhouses (or perhaps cattle minders' or shepherds' huts) on the Big Moor above the Bar Brook found shelter below a shelf and were surrounded by small yards or plots no bigger than gardens that were enclosed by stone walls. Excavation of one of the 'hut circles' revealed the stone footings of a dwelling that had probably been built of timber and roofed with thatch or turves. It was 20 feet in diameter and had replaced a larger timber building, which was identified by its postholes. The artefacts that were found suggested that farming activities were supplemented by the manufacture of polished shale rings, some of which seem to have been bracelets. The stones that had been laboriously gathered over the years from the woodland clearances in order to create the small, irregular-shaped fields at Swine Sty were heaped together in cairns that are now hard to distinguish from the burial mounds of the same era. The inner cereal fields were probably ploughed with primitive wooden ards and harvested with bronze sickles, but in summertime flocks and herds grazed the surrounding uplands. Pollen analysis has revealed a considerable increase in the amount of grassland during the Bronze Age, so it seems likely that farming in this district was essentially pastoral.

Swine Sty was probably typical of many other sites on what are now the Eastern Moors. On Stoke Flat and Birchen Edge, for example, prehistoric

Excavations at this Bronze Age site at Swine Sty on the Big Moor have revealed the stone foundations of dwellings that were probably timber-framed and thatched. Cereals were grown in small fields, little bigger than gardens, and livestock grazed beyond. The making of polished stone rings and bracelets was a by-employment. This moorland landscape now looks inhospitable but it was farmed by numerous generations of prehistoric people before the peat began to spread.

earthen field boundaries that probably supported stock-proof hedges are still visible. Fields such as these were cultivated over a long span of time in the second and first millennium BC, but it is unclear whether the farmers lived at these altitudes throughout the year or just in the summer months. In his detailed surveys of all the available evidence, John Barnatt has argued that the sustained use of specific areas of land by small 'family' farms on the local gritstones may have developed at an earlier date than in parts of lowland Britain, and perhaps continued in use long after the creation of planned landscapes in districts such as Dartmoor. Each extended family or kin seems to have had a stone circle and a group of barrows containing multiple burials and simple grave goods near the edge of its fields, with woodland and rough pastures stretching beyond.

A little further south, the more sheltered and better-drained parts of Gibbet Moor, Beeley Warren, Beeley Moor and Gardom's Edge contain many similar earthworks. The stone foundations of roundhouses, scattered in isolation or in small groups amongst the fields, have survived but their wooden posts, wattle and daub walls, and turf or thatch roofs have gone. Eleven have been identified tentatively on the moors above Chatsworth and twenty-four prehistoric agricultural areas have been recognised there from clearance heaps and occasional earthen banks and lynchets. On Beeley Warren, archaeological remains have been found in three discrete areas, each with its own field boundaries and monuments.

The most common prehistoric monuments on the moors are the round barrows. For instance, at least thirty-three examples have been found on the Chatsworth estate in surveys led by John Barnatt, including three within the park. Many others have no doubt been removed by centuries of later farming activities. An exceptionally well-preserved barrow on Gardom's Edge is topped by three eighteenth-century cairns known as the Three Men of Gardom's, which according to an unlikely legend commemorate the death of three shepherds or perhaps three priests. Most barrows have simple circular mounds built of stone and earth. The most unusual one is Hob Hurst's House on Harland Edge, where a square central mound is retained by a drystone wall and surrounded by an outer bank and ditch. It was excavated by Thomas Bateman in 1853. Another square-shaped barrow stands further east at Rod Knoll.

Many of the largest surviving Bronze Age round barrows stand dramatically on hill tops or ridges. In the Middle Ages they tended to acquire fanciful names such as Lord's Seat on Rushup Edge above Edale. Hallamshire examples include Pike Lowe, high on Midhope Moors, and Crow Chin, on the Stanage escarpment. Dozens of small barrows and clearance cairns can be seen on Hallam Moors near the Headstone after the heather has been burnt.

In Staffordshire many of the numerous Bronze Age barrows in Alstonefield are sited at the highest points in the local landscape and are often commemorated by the place-name 'low', from the Old English word *hlaw*, meaning a burial mound, as in Warslow. The north-eastern boundary of Onecote township was marked by a barrow called Merryton Low, the burial mound at the mere or border. At Fawfieldhead four Bronze Age barrows have been identified near a farmhouse called the Low, and in Leek township Cock Low, which was recorded as Catteslowe in the later sixteenth century, produced a Bronze Age cremation urn when it was destroyed in 1907. In Rushton Spencer township in the parish of Leek the boundary between Staffordshire and Cheshire runs

Pike Low, the highest point on Midhope Moors, was chosen as the site of a Bronze Age burial mound. Pike is a corruption of Peak and Low is derived from the common Anglo-Saxon word for a burial mound on a hill or ridge. The large cairn has been added in modern times.

along the top of an outcrop of rock known since at least Ancient British times as the Cloud. This border was marked in the early seventeenth century by a monolith called the Stepmother Stone and by a mound called Mystylowe, possibly the name used for the Neolithic chambered tomb now called the Bridestones on the Cheshire side of the boundary.

Some of these prehistoric barrows were re-used by much later people, who were perhaps staking a claim to the most ancient landmarks on the moorland edges. That at Steep Low contained, besides Bronze Age remains, an Anglian burial and Roman coins. Another at Stanshope had some Samian-ware from the Roman period.

The Peak District did not have rich and powerful chieftains like the men who dominated Bronze Age Wessex. Gold ornaments are absent from the local barrows, whose character and distribution strongly suggest that they were built by ordinary farming families. On the Eastern Moors all the stone circles, ringcairns and stone settings are found within or very close to the settlements and their surrounding fields. Most of the local round barrows are only 10 to 20 metres in diameter. The largest can often be seen from afar, erect on ridges as markers of the lands of various groups of families. They were sometimes enlarged or modified at a later stage when new burials were inserted, and they seem to have been left without cover for long periods of time before a stone and grass mound was erected over the bones, perhaps as a symbolic act to close the site down.

Much of what we know about Bronze Age people comes from their burial practices, though some of the many ways in which they dealt with their dead have left little or no trace on the ground. A cemetery near the Eagle Stone, on the Eastern Moors high above Baslow, was found by chance when a new drainage ditch provided an opportunity to excavate. The archaeologists unearthed the cremated ashes of fifteen women and children, which were contained in pots that had been placed in small pits or else deposited straight into the earth. Other finds included an intact funeral pyre and the remains of several other pyres nearby, and funerary goods that included stone tools, a perforated antler plate, faience beads and a bone whistle in a small urn that contained the cremated ashes of a child. Next to the cemetery, clearance cairns, house platforms and field walls demonstrated at least eight phases of occupation, extending over several hundred years. How many other stretches of moorland, we wonder, contain secrets such as these?

The grandest ritual monuments in Derbyshire are found on the limestone plateau of the White Peak, but the surrounding gritstone moorlands have a large number of small stone circles, dating mostly from the Earlier Bronze Age rather than the late Neolithic era. Fine examples can be seen on Stanton Moor, Beeley Moor, the Eastern Moors and Eyam, Abney, Offerton, Bamford and Broomhead Moors. They range in diameter from 15 to 100 feet, and are similar in style to monuments in many parts of northern and western England and southern Scotland. Stone circles were aligned roughly on the setting or rising sun at the solstices, but we can only imagine the variety of ceremonies that may have taken place there. A typical circle is formed by a ring of stones of various shapes and sizes no more than 2 or 3 feet high, with one or two entrances, and sometimes a single upright beyond. Every circle has lost some of its stones, while those known as ringcairns have none at all and perhaps never did. Excavations of the interiors of a few circles have produced evidence of human cremations, sometimes in urns. On the gritstone moorlands around the River Derwent cremated remains were often placed in a type of urn that was distinguished by its 'collared' or 'overhanging' rim and sealed with flat stones. Large numbers have been found among the barrows, ringcairns and stone circles on Stanton Moor, together with similar vessels that were used for storing food. At Wet Wythens

The Seven Stones circle on Bamford Moor. Numerous small stone circles are scattered around the gritstone moors. They are often difficult to find amongst the heather or bracken.

on Eyam Moor, where ten of the original sixteen stones remain standing, a Middle Bronze Age cremation urn was buried in the centre of the circle.

One of the best-preserved Bronze Age sites in England stands on the 1,000-feet high plateau of Stanton Moor, a ritual landscape overlooking the cultivated Derwent and Wye valleys. Prehistoric people did not live or farm there. Instead, they set it apart in memory of their ancestors. Numerous cremation urn cemeteries are known from excavation and no less than five stone circles or ringcairns and over seventy barrows can be traced amongst the heather and the silver birch. The best-known stone circle has been dubbed the Nine Ladies, though a tenth stone has been found and another probably filled the remaining gap. Associated with it is the King Stone that stands apart, some 40 metres to the south-west. Old drawings depict a central cairn and a bank on which the stones were placed, but these features have been trodden down by a regular stream of visitors.

The spread of bracken, heather and birch trees makes it difficult to find two more circles that stand nearby. The largest is known as the Central and is classified as a ringcairn, for we cannot tell whether or not it ever had standing stones.

Cremation urns and simple grave goods were discovered during the excavation of the smallest circle at Doll Tor, which has six standing stones and a later cairn at the eastern end. The special atmosphere of Stanton Moor is enhanced by some striking natural rocks, especially the Andle or Anvil Stone, which dominates the landscape close to Doll Tor, and the Cork Stone, which is over 10 feet high and was once surrounded by four standing stones. Many of the barrows occupy striking positions on the skyline in order to be seen from below. This is a truly exceptional place.

Another extraordinary site on a gritstone shelf known as Gardom's Edge towers above the road that descends from Owler Bar to Baslow. It was excavated in the early 1990s and ascribed initially to the late Neolithic era, but radiocarbon dates have now placed it in the later Bronze Age. A massive stone bank, 3 to 5 feet high in parts and between 16 and 30 feet wide, stretches back from the edge of the precipice to form a 15-acre, D-shaped enclosure. Most of its interior is strewn with boulders, so it is unlikely that it was lived in, nor does the wide but low bank that stops before it reaches the scarp edge suggest a communal stock enclosure. Few burial sites have been identified and the surrounding land could not have supported a large population. It seems, therefore, that people must have come from miles around to build it and to use it as a focal place for seasonal gatherings.

Gardom's Edge occupies a commanding position that overlooks the deep valley of the Bar Brook as it joins the wider valley of the Derwent and provides clear views of the White Peak in the distance. The landscape has been shaped in many periods, but most of the 1,300 archaeological finds are prehistoric. Extensive remains of field boundaries, clearance cairns, house sites and monuments from the later Bronze Age can be seen beyond the edge-top enclosure, stretching up towards Birchen Edge, where the land was subsequently used for rough grazing. But on the southern slopes, farming activities over numerous generations have probably destroyed similar sites. The foundations of prehistoric timber-framed houses amongst the fields can be recognised, often on platforms that were levelled into the hillside. One of the most spectacular finds was the best-preserved example of prehistoric cup-and-ring marks that has so far been discovered in the Peak District. The exact purpose and date of such patterns and linear designs remain debatable, but they often appear in the north of England alongside important paths and field boundaries, perhaps as signs or markers of territories.

In the later Bronze Age an extraordinary new form of settlement was created on the windy summit of Mam Tor. Many of the 100 or more platforms that were cut into the hillsides have been shown by excavation to have supported roundhouses. Even if we allow that not all the platforms were

A massive stone bank forms a half-circle back from the steep escarpment of Gardom's Edge near Baslow, with entrances at various points. When the site was excavated in the 1990s it was thought to be Neolithic but radiocarbon dating now suggests that the wall and associated monuments were erected in the late Bronze Age to enclose a huge ceremonial area.

contemporary, the settlement was unusually large and persistent. Charcoal obtained from the foundations of some of these dwellings has provided radiocarbon dates from the centuries around 1350 BC, and many later Bronze Age artefacts, including an abundance of pottery, together with several shale bracelets and a polished stone axe, have been discovered. The remains of two Bronze Age barrows on the edge of the summit yielded a bronze axe and a cinerary urn. The exposed position of the settlement and the lack of nearby arable land indicate the special nature of the site, which must have relied on a large catchment area, stretching down into the Hope and Edale valleys and onto the limestone plateau. The ramparts that enclose the settlement on Mam Tor have not been dated but they are thought to have been a later development in the Iron Age, when Mam Tor was converted into a hill fort.

Elsewhere, the Peak District moors have yielded only sporadic evidence of Bronze Age activity. For example, the remains of settlements and fields in the Upper Derwent Valley are fragmentary and relatively few barbed and tanged arrowheads have been found on Meltham Moor and Wessenden

Head. A group of cairns and banks in the area between Honley and Holmfirth suggests that extensive Bronze Age settlements may have existed there. But a bronze spearhead found on Cartworth Moor in 1811 and some arrowheads are the only artefacts that have been discovered in this region. The poor soils and heavy rainfall of these moorland districts would have discouraged farmers, and the flint arrowheads suggest that it was still necessary to increase the food supply by hunting. Yet the Bronze Age fields may not have been abandoned until soils deteriorated and peat began to spread when the climate worsened in the first millennium BC.

About 1500 BC the rituals in the stone circles came to an end and special cemeteries such as those on Stanton Moor were no longer used. We cannot say why, but perhaps it no longer seemed appropriate to assert communal grazing rights once a growing population had divided the landscape between different owners. Yet the Peak District seems to have lacked the tribal leaders and the great linear earthworks of contemporary Yorkshire or Wessex. The later Bronze Age has left few burial sites, artefacts are usually discovered only in isolation, metalwork is rarely found, and the pottery cannot be placed in clear sequences. Perhaps climate change was responsible for this apparent decline of economic, social and ceremonial activities, for Britain became cooler and wetter, with average temperatures 2°C lower than today. Faced with increased demands from the rising population, the shallow soils over the gritstones lost their fertility and the growing of cereals was abandoned when peat began to spread over the arable lands. The uplands became used only for pasture and farmsteads were deserted when families moved to new sites that were cleared from the woods in the river valleys below.

The Iron Age

Few changes in the landscape are evident anywhere in Britain in the first phase of the Iron Age between 700 and 500 BC, but from then onwards new sites and finds of artefacts increase markedly. Woodland was reduced dramatically and permanently and the population soared. The most obvious lasting features are the range of earthworks that are classified together, rather unsatisfactorily, as hill forts. These range from the mighty, defended site at Mam Tor, the only hill fort in the Peak District that is known throughout the land, to small enclosures that may have been created just to impound livestock. Mam Tor can be seen from miles around, soaring above Edale and the Hope Valley. The inhabitants of the fort, who must surely have formed the local ruling elite, had ready access to a variety of resources where the limestone plateau meets the gritstone uplands. Sixteen acres were enclosed within a single, stone-revetted rampart, with a ditch and counterscarp bank that follow the contours around the hog-back of the hill. The defences are well-preserved, except on the eastern side of 'the shivering mountain', where they have been destroyed by landslip. The site is entered by narrow passages at the main entrance in the south-west corner and at a smaller entry at the northern end. We do not know how long the hill fort was in use, but Mam Tor remained the major focal point in the Peak District for much of the first millennium BC. Its nearest rival of comparable size and date was many miles further north at Castle Hill, Almondbury.

A much smaller hill fort of 2½ acres, known as Castle Naze, forms the northern end of Coombs Moss to the south of Chapel-en-le-Frith. Two of its three sides are defended by steep natural slopes, but the other has a deep ditch and double ramparts that stretch about 550 feet across the promontory with a causewayed entrance in the middle. An even smaller D-shaped enclosure, just over an acre in size, at Oldfield Hill, south-west of Meltham, is defined by a rampart and an outer ditch. It was originally thought to be a Roman fort, but the accepted opinion now is that it was a well-defended Iron Age farmstead with two stages of construction and some evidence of iron working. Two similar sites, each referred to as 'castles', are

Mam Tor was first settled in the Bronze Age, but the impressive ramparts around the summit are characteristic of the Iron Age, when Mam Tor was a tribal capital.

now barely discernible on the great ridge to the south of Penistone. Several other contemporary earthworks are found in the White Peak.

In the late 1990s an important Iron Age site was discovered near the parish church at Mellor, on the north-western edge of the Peak District, where an enclosing ditch 6 feet deep and 4 metres wide had been cut through the underlying rock. Fragments of Roman tile, pottery and glass were found in the upper layers, but underneath were Iron Age potsherds and broken pieces of crucibles that had been used for casting bronze. Charcoal from near the base of the ditch provided a radiocarbon date from the fifth century BC. Then an almost-complete Iron Age pot, shaped in clay slabs without the use of a wheel, was unearthed nearby and dated to 520–380 BC. This was an important find as so little pottery survives in the Peak District from this era. The next discoveries were an Iron Age roundhouse and another deep ditch, which suggested a double system of boundaries, then many more roundhouses that were identified by their postholes. The hill fort or settlement may have been abandoned before it was re-occupied by the Romans. The discovery of Samian-ware, glass and some fine brooches suggests that a Roman building stood close-by from the first to the third century AD.

We know less about the Iron Age inhabitants of the moorlands than we do about their ancestors. On the Eastern Moors many of the old fields remained in use until the climate worsened, the soils deteriorated and the advance of the peat became unstoppable. Peat consists of the piled-up remains of centuries of dead plants. Where the ground is permanently wet, these plants do not rot. Instead, they accumulate on the surface in a black or dark brown layer above the mineral soil. The high rainfall that causes blanket peat to form also washes out the minerals. The impression that we get from the available evidence is that the population increased on the flanks of the moors and many new farms were created there, but the uplands were now used mainly for the grazing of livestock in the summer months. The soils could no longer support the cultivation of cereals. Archaeological investigations and pollen analyses have shown that the timescale of this change to a pastoral economy varied from one area to another, but by the end of the Iron Age all the large moors in the Peak District had been formed. However, they were not as extensive as they are now, for much of their edges were still farmed and some wildwood survived.

The moors were created in prehistoric times from both natural causes and human activities. The leaching of soils and the formation of peat turned large areas of wildwood into moorland, and in some areas human activities quickened these processes. At high altitudes with heavy rainfalls, such as on Bleaklow and Kinder Scout, the moors are a natural phenomenon. There is little evidence that prehistoric families penetrated there for long. When blanket-peat began to accumulate, wildwood survived precariously only in favoured localities. In other districts, however, the peat probably spread more quickly after farmers felled the trees. Most of the drier, less peaty areas, like the Eastern Moors, would probably still be covered with woods today had humans not intervened. Such places were well-populated in prehistoric times and crops were grown at much higher elevations than would now be thought possible. Yet even here, cultivation was short lived. As the soils became leached of their minerals, the sowing of crops was curtailed and the land was turned to pasture. When blanket-bog spread downhill, the farmsteads were abandoned.

Moorland is a distinctive type of British vegetation, but there is much variety from one moor to another. Heather is the most characteristic plant, yet other moors are dominated by grasses and bracken, by soft rushes, bog-myrtle and crowberry, and in the wetter parts by sphagnum moss and lichens and by bogs in the valleys. The drier moorlands in the east are similar to heaths, with only an inch or two of peat, but on Kinder Scout and other northern moors the peat can be many feet thick.

Romans, Angles and Vikings

The Roman Army arrived in the Peak District in the late 70s or 80s AD and quickly established forts that were linked by military roads. The two that were nearest to the moors were erected to control significant routes across the hills. *Navio* was built at the confluence of the river Noe and the Bradwell Brook, as a successor to Mam Tor, the former guardian of the route down the Winnats Pass. In later times it was commemorated by the Anglo-Saxon name Brough. Both the route from *Navio* to Manchester and the Pennine crossing through Longdendale were guarded by a fort on a 3½-acre spur that overlooked the confluence of the River Etherow and the Glossop Brook. Its Roman name is uncertain but may have been *Erdotalia*, meaning 'on the ridge overlooking the Etherow', whose British name was *Edera*. 'Melandra Castle' was an eighteenth-century antiquarian's invention. The main approach was from the south, for the ground falls away steeply on the other three sides. The wooden buildings of the early fort, enclosed by a turf-covered earth rampart and a ditch, were replaced by stone structures when the fort was rebuilt in the 120s. Finds from excavations include a carved altar stone and an inscription noting the presence of the First Cohort of Frisiavonians, who were also based at Manchester.

A 5-acre *vicus* that formed a commercial and domestic area on the southern and south-eastern sides of the fort was enclosed within its own rampart and ditch, beyond which lay the cemetery, alongside the road to the baths at Buxton. Much of it is now covered by a housing estate in Gamesley. The timber-framed accommodation included a guesthouse measuring 150 by 60 feet, which seems to have been demolished about 140, when all signs of occupation come to an end. Unlike *Navio*, Melandra Castle does not seem to have been re-occupied in the 150s, but coins have been found there that date from the late-third and fourth centuries.

The only other Roman fort on the Peak District moors was a small one in the north-west for about 500 auxiliary troops. This was constructed of turf and timber about AD 79 on Castle Hill, on the edge of Castleshaw and at the foot of Standedge, in order to guard the road from York to Chester via Slack and Manchester. The foundations of the headquarters, commander's tent, granary, stables and six long narrow buildings thought to have been workshops or storerooms have been located. The fort fell out of use in the 90s, but about 105 was replaced by a turf-and-timber fortlet. Gates, barracks, commander's house, a courtyard building, granary, workshop, a hypocaust, an oven, a well and possibly a latrine have been identified from a second construction phase about 105. As the barracks could have accommodated only forty-eight soldiers, the total garrison must have numbered less than 100. A civilian settlement or *vicus* grew around the fortlet in the early second century, but both fell out of use in the mid-120s. Sections of the road between Slack and Castleshaw have been excavated or surveyed on the way to the Colne Valley and Marsden and up to a small, first-century military station on the slopes of Pule Hill.

The military roads that connected the forts formed only a small part of the network of routes that linked the scattered farms of the native British, including those on the edges of the moors. Roman soldiers and administrators were stationed in the Peak District because of the lucrative lead mines. They had little interest in the moorlands and their presence was hardly felt there. The native Britons continued to farm their land in much the same way as their Iron Age ancestors had done. Iron ploughs turned over the better soils, but the moors were used only for the summer grazing of livestock by those farmers who lived on the fringes. Traces of a rare survival of a Romano-British farming hamlet can be found at the Warren between North Lees and the Stanage escarpment in the parish of Hathersage. The foundations of both a roundhouse and rectangular buildings can be observed on terraces that were cut into the slope and revetted with gritstone boulders. Elsewhere, low earthen lynchets formed field boundaries within the stony ground.

The oldest surviving names in the English landscape are mostly those of rivers. The Colne, Derwent, Don, Dove, Goyt and Noe are either Celtic or pre-Celtic names. A few other Celtic words are preserved in topographical features, especially the hills of different shapes that have produced such diverse names as Crook Hill, Kinder, Mellor and Penistone, together with the numerous tors and the series of 'bar' names for gritstone edges such as Baslow Bar. About half of Derbyshire's Celtic names are found in the north-western uplands. The Ancient British era is also commemorated by a

Most native British sites from the Roman period have been obliterated by later farming activities, but on the moorland fringe above North Lees chapel, Hathersage, the earthworks of a complete settlement and its adjoining fields, including walls that still stand three courses high, can be seen amidst the bracken below Stanage Edge.

handful of *Eccles* names that tell of the existence of Christian communities and churches in late Roman times. Eccles House stands close to the Roman fort at *Navio*, half-a-mile from the church at Hope whose enormous parish stretched over the moorlands. Another Eccles House on the northern side of Eccles Pike, a dramatic peak near Chapel-en-le-Frith, suggests a similar early foundation, and across the Yorkshire boundary Ecclesfield church – known by the seventeenth century as 'The Minster of the Moors' – served the whole of the ancient district known as Hallamshire.

The lack of documentary and archaeological evidence between the Roman and Norman periods inhibits our understanding of the moorland economy before the thirteenth century. Even Domesday Book is silent about the moors, which can be deduced only as gaps between settlements. Pollen analysis indicates that the climate deteriorated from the late Roman period onwards and that increased rainfall and frequent floods encouraged the spread of shallow acid peat over large areas of woodland. A marked decline

The river Derwent starts its course high in the Peak District, where it still forms the boundary between Derbyshire (left) and Yorkshire. Its Ancient British name means 'abounding in oaks', though the wooded landscape would have been more obvious much further downstream.

in the level of population hastened the retreat from the moors and some woodland regeneration, but pollen samples taken from wet areas such as Featherbed Moss and Leash Fen indicate renewed woodland clearance in the late Anglo-Scandinavian period.

Ancient British tribes controlled the Peak District until the Angles advanced into the hills in the mid-seventh century. Then, the ruling elites were replaced but the farming population remained native. A large number of Anglian place-names and field-names contain the element *hlaw*, which could mean simply a mound or a hill, but in the Peak District it usually had the more precise meaning of burial mound. These burial sites are found particularly in the White Peak, where Bronze Age barrows were re-used by the leaders of the Anglian army. A more unusual sight, a mile or two north-west of Wincle, near the road from Buxton to Congleton, is Cluelow Cross, a round pillar about 10 feet high with the remains of a small wheelhead cross on the top. This Christian symbol was erected in the late Mercian period in the middle of of a large and prominent prehistoric barrow, now set in a small plantation.

The northern part of the Peak District has a sizeable collection of place-names ending in -*worth*, meaning a small enclosure. Buxworth, Charlesworth, Chisworth, Hollinworth, Ludworth and Rowarth form a group of *worth* names in north-west Derbyshire that number as many as in the rest of the county together. Hallamshire has Dungworth, Hawksworth, Holdworth and Sugworth; and further north we find Cartworth, Hepworth and Saddleworth. The ancient estates that included the moorlands were administered from centres that were sited away from the moors. Their place-names often ended with the element -*feld*, meaning open countryside cleared from the surrounding woodlands, a term that has produced such names as Alstonefield, Bradfield, Chesterfield, Dronfield, Ecclesfield, Holmesfield, Macclesfield and Sheffield.

The fluctuating fortunes of the two major groups of Anglians – the Mercians and the Northumbrians – meant that their border often changed before county boundaries were established. The *Anglo-Saxon Chronicle* twice suggests that Dore marked this boundary in the ninth and tenth centuries. In a symbolic gesture in 828 the Northumbrians crossed the frontier to agree terms with the victorious army of Egbert of Wessex. In 942 Edmund, son of Edward the Elder, conquered the Danes of Mercia and became ruler 'as far as Dore divides'. The place-name means a 'narrow pass', or literally a door.

An ancient list known as the *Tribal Hidage* names the tribes or small kingdoms that paid tribute to the Mercians, or perhaps with Mercia to the

Northumbrians. One of the groups on the northern edge of the Mercian heartland was known as the *Pecsaetan*, whose territory was recorded as *Pecsaetna lond*, 'the land of the settlers of the Peak'. The *Anglo-Saxon Chronicle* for 920 referred to Bakewell as being in *Peac lond* and a charter of 963 described Ballidon as being 'in the district of the *Pecsaetan*', so their territory extended over both the High Peak and the Low Peak to include the whole of what we now know as the Peak District. The *Pecsaetan* were probably native people who long retained their identity under Anglo-Scandinavian lords. They seem to have been the ancestors of the *Peakrills*, the derogatory name given to the local inhabitants 1,000 years later.

The Anglian kingdom of Northumbria was divided into territories known as shires. In the extreme south-west of the kingdom Hallamshire covered the 71,526 acres that formed the parish of Ecclesfield and the chapelries of Bradfield and Sheffield and it extended over large stretches of moorland as far north as the Little Don and the River Etherow, and as far west as the River Derwent, which formed the county boundary with Derbyshire. Watercourses, groups of rocks twisted into grotesque shapes by wind, rain and ice, and manmade crosses and poles acted as the boundary points. Even today, Stanedge Pole is a dramatic reminder of this ancient boundary between the two great Anglo-Saxon kingdoms of Northumbria and Mercia and between the archbishoprics of York and Canterbury. Detached portions of parishes are not found beyond the boundary line, no churches or chapels paid any sort of dues to mother churches across the boundary, and no manorial jurisdictions crossed the frontier. This was a real and lasting division of the land.

Neither the Angles nor the Vikings made much impact on the management

Stanedge Pole. A long succession of poles set into a prominent rock marked the moorland county boundary between Yorkshire and Derbyshire. In Anglo-Saxon times this was also the boundary between the kingdoms of Northumbria and Mercia. It served too as the ecclesiastical boundary between York and Canterbury and the manorial boundary between Hallamshire and Hathersage.

of the Peak District moors. No Scandinavian place-names ending in *-by* or *-thwaite* appear there, though a few *-thorpe* endings for outlying settlements on the edges are evident in such names as Cutthorpe, Jordanthorpe and Millthorpe, and the Vikings have influenced the forms of only a few other names, such as Crookes, Hazlebadge, Holmesfield, Onesacre, Thurlstone and Ughill. Old Norse words that passed into local speech include booth (cattle-rearing farm), gate (road) and grain (a small valley forking off another), and in the parish of Sheffield the townships of Brightside and Ecclesall were known as bierlows. But all this does not amount to much. By the late Anglo-Scandinavian period, however, the moors were all incorporated within the lordships and parishes that become familiar to us later in the Middle Ages.

The Peak District moorland landscape acquired its present form long before the Norman Conquest. It had degenerated into peat bogs, poor grassland and heaths, with narrow belts of wood surviving in the steep valleys. The grazing of the moors in the summer months by cattle and sheep that had spent the winter in the surrounding lowlands prevented the regeneration of birch and other small trees such as rowan. Otherwise, the moors were visited only for the digging of peat and the occasional gathering of wood, gorse, bracken and roofing materials.

The Wainstones, or Wheelstones, on Derwent Edge marked the boundary of Hallamshire in the thirteenth century.

Chapter 3

The Middle Ages

Forests, chases and lordships

The Norman kings and barons turned huge stretches of the English countryside, including much of the Pennine moorlands, into royal forests or private chases for hunting deer and other game such as hares or wild boars. 'Forest' was not used in the present sense of a thick wood, but as a legal term for a district that was subject to a special set of harsh laws imposed by forest courts and officers of the Crown. The term was derived from the Latin word *foris*, implying an area that lay outside the reach of English common law. The woods that had once stretched over the Peak District had long since gone. A 'chase', which was sometimes otherwise known as a 'frith' or 'firth', was a baron's equivalent to a royal forest. The boundaries of these moorland forests and chases were marked by streams, prominent rocks and sometimes by stone crosses, but as hunting was only an occasional activity, the more fertile parts were set aside for growing crops and grazing cattle, sheep, pigs and horses. The lords found that it was profitable to allow peasant farmers to clear new fields on the edges of the moors on the payment of entry fines and annual rents. Forests and chases therefore contained cultivated fields, farmsteads, cottages, hamlets and sometimes even villages and small market centres within their bounds, but stern laws preserved the lord's hunting rights, imposed severe penalties on poachers, and ordered the maiming of dogs so that they could not chase the game.

The Royal Forest of the Peak
In 1155 a huge tract of land covering 180 square miles of limestone and gritstone moors in north-west Derbyshire, which formed part of the honour or lordship of the Norman baron William Peveril, was forfeited to the Crown and soon became known as the Royal Forest of the Peak. When its bounds were first recorded in 1286 this forest stretched from the River Derwent in the east to the River Goyt in the west, and from the River Wye in the south

to the River Etherow in the north. The western and northern boundaries of the forest coincided with the border between Derbyshire and Cheshire.

Peak Castle at Castleton was the administrative and legal centre for the forest and the prison for offenders. In the mid–1250s Gervase de Bernake, the forest bailiff, built and endowed a chapel, which in time became the church of Peak Forest, with a 'peculiar jurisdiction' outside the parish system. The hunting lodge was on or near the site of Chamber Farm, 'the chamber in the forest', whose successor stands on a knoll just north of the present village of Peak Forest. In the thirteenth and fourteenth centuries the minor courts or 'swainmotes' for Campana ward were held at this Chamber, whereas those for Longdendale met at Bowden, near Chapel-en-le-Frith, and those for Hopedale met at Hope. By the early thirteenth century the officers of the Forest of the Peak lived mostly in and around Bowden, 3 miles north-west of their headquarters at Chamber Farm. In about 1225 they built their own place of worship there and gave it the name of Chapel-en-le-Frith, the chapel in the forest.

The hereditary officers who held their land in return for discharging specific duties included those with the distinctive occupational surnames of Archer, Forester and Wolfhunt. The Wolfhunts set traps for the wolves in spring and autumn and hunted them with their trained mastiffs. Wolves remained within the Forest of the Peak until Tudor times and their memory was preserved in the minor place-names of Woolow, Wolf's Pit, Wooler and the lost Wolfstone (Hope Woodlands). Robert the Archer, who witnessed a deed dating from before 1214, founded a gentry family that became lords of Abney, Highlow and Hucklow. Other forester families also prospered over

Edale Cross is thought to have marked the medieval boundaries of the three wards of the Forest in the Peak. It stands at the summit of the bridleway from Edale to Hayfield via Jacob's Ladder, where it was re-erected in 1810 by John Gee and four other men, whose initials are inscribed on the top.

the generations. The Bagshaws, who took their name from a hamlet near Chapel-en-le-Frith, became lords of Wormhill and Abney. The Balguys, who lived at Aston in the twelfth century, were still wealthy at the end of the seventeenth century when Henry Balguy built Derwent Hall. The Eyres spread from Thornhill and Hope and acquired the manors of Padley and Hassop. The Foljambes started at Wormhill and Tideswell and by the end of the thirteenth century were knights of the shire. And the Woodroffes became a gentry family with land in Wormhill, Hope and Great Hucklow.

As the kings of England were infrequent visitors to the Forest of the Peak the officers had plenty of opportunities to enrich themselves illegally by killing deer, grazing their own sheep and cattle on the forest pastures, breeding large numbers of horses, and felling the woods. They were sometimes caught red-handed. In the early 1230s, for example, the bailiff, Ralph Bugge, a prosperous High Peak lead merchant, was fined for keeping sixty cart horses and four yoke of oxen on the pastures, to the detriment of the royal herds of deer. More lowly men who farmed within the forest or beyond its edges also took the law into their own hands. An enquiry in 1251 found that 131 people had built new houses without licence in the forest since the previous enquiry in 1216. At the same time, the forest officers had licensed the construction of 127 new houses so that the forest now had villages surrounded by open fields and even a few market centres. Royal charters were granted for weekly markets and annual fairs within the forest at Tideswell (1251), Chapel-en-le-Frith (1254), Glossop (1290) and Charlesworth (1328).

The Forest of the Peak eventually came under the jurisdiction of the Duchy of Lancaster, which was created in 1351 when Henry, Earl of Lancaster, was made a duke, and was revived in 1377 by a grant to John of Gaunt, second Duke of Lancaster, the father of the future King Henry IV. Even after it became a Crown estate again in 1399, the Duchy kept its distinctive judicial and administrative structure. During the fifteenth century its officers gave up stock farming and rented out their cattle and sheep farms and horse studs to Derbyshire gentry families: the Vernons, Bradburnes, Okeovers, Babingtons, Knivetons and others. However, they retained one-third of the 1,500-acre common pasture at Fairfield and 100 acres of waste in Mainstonefield, around the present Mainstone Farm, east of Chinley Head.

The fifteenth-century national economy underwent a series of booms and slumps but recovered in the 1470s. The value of extensive moorland pastures rose when meat and wool began to fetch high prices. This is reflected in the rentals of the five cattle-rearing booths or vaccaries of Edale, which increased by over twenty per cent between 1485 and 1520, and by the numerous bitter complaints against the unscrupulous men who tried to overstock the commons or to enclose parts of them. In 1516, for example, John Wellys (receiver of the honour of Tutbury) and Arthur Eyre were appointed as commissioners to enquire into complaints about the overstocking of the pastures of Campana ward. On a visit to the forest they saw about 360 deer but concluded that the grass was so bare from grazing by 960–980 cattle, some 4,000 sheep and 130 horses that the deer were not likely to last through the winter. One of the witnesses, Hugh Netham, aged 30, said on oath that five herds of cattle roamed the forest whereas only two had been allowed before. The commissioners recommended the removal of the sheep and the marking of the royal deer, but the problem was not solved until the number of deer was reduced later in the century when the fashion for hunting them declined.

Local landowners grabbed the opportunities presented by the Duchy's leases. In 1491–92 the account of Sir George Savage, bailiff of the High

Upper Booth, the most westerly of the Edale booths, nestles below Kinder Scout. In the Middle Ages these booths were used for rearing young cattle before they were fattened on lusher pastures elsewhere, but sheep are now more important and Upper Booth has a camp site.

Peak, noted that Henry Vernon had a ten-year lease at an annual £31.13s.4d. rent of 'the herbage of Crook Hill recently of the Abbot of Welbeck which has come into the king's hands by exchange for the herbage of Bristall which he has at farm from the nuns of Derby'. In 1497 John Savage, esquire, held a twenty-year lease of the pasture at Alport and Sir Edmund Trafford leased the Edale cattle-rearing booths, including those tenanted by John Barbour and Richard Barbour, whose surname is commemorated by Barber Booth. The other Edale booths are still known as Upper, Nether, Grindsbrook and Ollerbrook. In 1505–8 that part of the Upper Derwent Valley around Crookhill that lay within the Duchy of Lancaster included the booth at 'Rowsley alias Ronkesley', while the pastures at 'Ashop, Crymylkarre, Chappelleghside, Pedderhagge, Obholmes and Feireholmes, Alport' were tenanted by Sir Thomas Wortley of Wortley Hall, across the border in South Yorkshire. These wealthy graziers kept flocks of up to 400 sheep to provide wool for commercial markets. Meanwhile, the inventories of personal estates that were attached to wills in the 1530s show that ordinary peasant farmers kept small flocks of sheep and herds of beef cattle in many parts of the uplands, within or just outside the forest.

Other forests
The terms forest and chase were used somewhat loosely when ownership changed. Macclesfield Forest belonged to the Earls of Chester and covered the east Cheshire moorlands up to the boundary with the Forest of the Peak. First recorded in the twelfth century, when it was linked with the earl's forest of Leek, Macclesfield Forest appears to have been a pre-Conquest hunting estate of the Earls of Mercia. Domesday Book records that Earl Edwin had seven 'hays', which have been interpreted as park-like enclosures, and an extensive stretch of woodland, 'six leagues long and three wide'. As usual, however, the extent of the moorland was not recorded. Under the Normans, the forest was administered from Toot Hill, a dry-moated platform dug out of the underlying rock high up on the edge of the Pennines. The office of chief forester was regarded as hereditary by the Davenport family, and the seven under-sheriffs followed their chief's example by bequeathing their lucrative posts to their sons. Hunting seems to have been concentrated at the Coombs, where enclosures for deer were in place by 1291 and a hunting lodge was recorded in 1347. In 1303 it was reported that a machine had been made to catch wolves that were killing deer within the forest.

During the thirteenth century Macclesfield Forest began to change from a game preserve to a pasture for livestock. The Earls of Chester had horse studs and specialised cattle-rearing farms within the forest, where foals and calves were reared for sale at the markets and fairs in Macclesfield. By the fourteenth century the earls had also constructed two iron forges within the forest and the tenants, who held their lands by customary tenure, had the right to cut oaks and to clear new land upon payment of fines and rents. When Edward, the Black Prince, became lord of the manor in 1347, he determined to raise revenues and increase the number of livestock, but Paul Booth has shown that the accounts for 1356–76 reveal that the prince's projects were only moderately successful, for the labour shortage that followed the Black Death meant that wages rose by fifty per cent and continuous bad weather made a high proportion of cows barren and caused a high death rate amongst calves. The herd of 700 cattle fell by half in the mid-1370s and no one could be persuaded to take a lease to rear them. But the situation began to improve and by the mid-fifteenth century the entire estate was in the hands of tenants. In 1442 the major pastures at Saltersford, Harrop, Tod's Cliff, Wildboarclough, Midgley and Shutlingsloe were leased to Sir Thomas Stanley, whose family continued to profit from them for about 200 years.

In 1207 Ranulf, Earl of Chester, confirmed the weekly market and a seven-day annual fair at Leek, and by 1293 weekly markets and annual fairs were held in the chapelry of Longnor. The exact extent of the earl's Leek Forest is uncertain, but it included the townships of Leekfrith and Rushton Spencer within the parish of Leek and a hunting ground at Hollinhay in Longsdon. Little is known about hunting in Leek Forest, but stock farming flourished in the twelfth and thirteenth centuries on the pastures of Morridge and the Churnet Valley, and by 1273 the income from the herbage and pannage of Horton Hay was nearly a third of the value of the whole manor of Horton. The Lord of Horton received a payment known as cowscot from farmers in neighbouring manors who pastured cattle there; for example, from 1278 the townships of Endon and Longsdon each paid twenty shillings every third year and Endon contributed an additional 2s.6d. every second year. Horton Hay was also exploited for its minerals. The iron forges that were recorded there in 1239 were still being worked in the early sixteenth century and coal was mined in shallow pits from at least the fourteenth century onwards.

Other parts of Staffordshire were included within Alstonefield Forest, which was first recorded in 1227 but was probably in existence by the twelfth century. It included the townships of Fawfieldhead, Heathylee, Hollinsclough and Quarnford and was sometimes known as the Forest of Maubun or as Malbank Frith or Firth, after the Malbank family, Lords of Alstonefield. As late as 1670 local people remembered that Malbon Firth

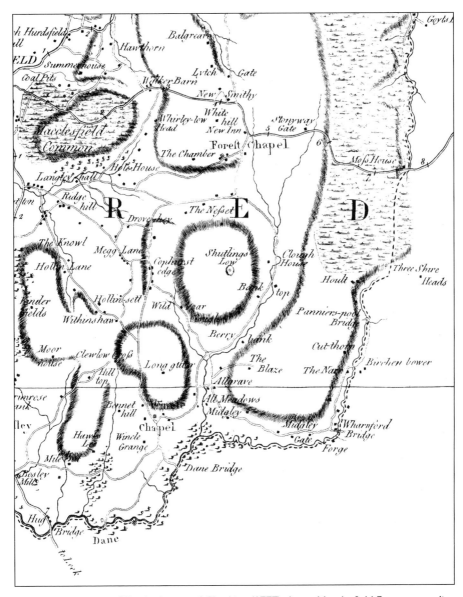

This eastern section of Burdett's map of Cheshire (1777) shows Macclesfield Forest extending across the hills (notably Shutlingsloe) and the moors to the county boundary in the east. The ancient route from Macclesfield to Buxton was made a turnpike road in 1759.

had once been stocked with deer. Surviving manorial accounts include payments to the lord for winter and summer 'agistment' (rents for pasturing livestock), and for the right to dig peat for fuel. Cattle-rearing farms, or vaccaries, were recorded at Fawfieldhead and Quarnford in the *inquisition post mortem* of Thomas de Audley in 1307, and local place-names recall the 'stalls' where tenant farmers reared cattle together with several places in Alstonefield parish, which were first occupied as outlying dairy farms.

On the other side of the Peak District, some time between 1154 and 1167, King Henry II designated the whole of Derbyshire east of the River Derwent (except Belper ward in Duffield Frith) as another royal forest. This covered an enormous area of 250 square miles that was mostly wood pasture but which included the Eastern Moors. It did not last long, however, for the forest organisation was dismantled in 1225, and it has left no permanent mark on the landscape and little documentary evidence in the Crown's records. Unlike the other moors of the southern Pennines, this large stretch of moorland between Matlock and Hallamshire was not designated for the hunting of deer, except for this brief period. It is ironic, then, that the largest herd of wild deer to graze the Peak District moors today are found on the Big Moor and Totley Moss.

Hallamshire

Hallamshire was the ancient name of a district that stretched across the moors of south-west Yorkshire to the county boundary marked by Stanedge Pole in the west. The Norman lords, the Lovetots and their successors the Furnivals, built Sheffield Castle and laid out a market place where the surplus produce of the farmers was sold. At the *Quo Warranto* enquiries into baronial privileges in 1281 Thomas de Furnival claimed that he and his ancestors had enjoyed the right to hunt in Hallamshire since the Conquest. They had enclosed an enormous deer park covering 2,461 acres on the other side of the River Sheaf from the castle and had created three extensive moorland chases or firths, known as Rivelin, Hawkesworth and Loxley. In 1637 the surveyor John Harrison measured the chase or firth in the Rivelin Valley at 6,863 acres.

Ughill, Holdworth, Onesacre and Worrall were recorded by name in the Domesday Book entry for Hallamshire, and other farmsteads or hamlets within the chapelry of Bradfield were probably included silently amongst the outlying *berewicks*. Families had settled close to the present edges of the local moors by late Anglo-Scandinavian times. The medieval freeholders and tenants of these farms were allowed to rent pastures and woodland grazings in the chases and on other parts of the moors, and manorial court rolls recorded rents for the manorial pastures in the deep valleys of Agden,

Ewden, Harden, Howden and Rivelin, and for 'holly sold there for the fodder of the animals in winter time'. In Rivelin Chase the lord received 'pasturing rents for divers plough-cattle on the moor from strangers there' and rents for 'the grinding wheels in the lord's quarry'. The reference to cattle belonging to 'strangers' suggests an annual summer migration from beyond the forest, but transhumance in the Peak District was on a much smaller scale than on Dartmoor.

In 1184 the Lord of Hallamshire had two cattle-rearing farms – Old Booth in the chapelry of Bradfield and Fulwood Booth in Rivelin Chase – which he restocked with forty cows, four bulls and eight oxen. Old Booth Farm is now a seventeenth-century building on the east side of Broomhead Moor and the present Fulwood Booth Farm stands on the moorland track that leads towards Stanedge Pole. The lord's servants still reared young beasts at Fulwood Booth in Elizabethan times, and the farm was described as a 123-acre pasture in the 1637 survey. Harrison also noted a 62-acre pasture nearby at Redmires, which was 'reserved for the Deare being Invironed within

St Nicholas's church served the huge moorland chapelry of Bradfield within the parish of Ecclesfield. It was erected at High Bradfield close to the motte-and-bailey castle of the Norman lords of Hallamshire (now hidden by the trees to the left). Low Bradfield developed around the manorial corn mill in the valley below. In the late Middle Ages the church was rebuilt in a fine Perpendicular Gothic style.

Rivelin Firth'. The owners of the various sub-manors within Hallamshire also had hunting rights on their estates, which sometimes extended across the moors. Elias de Midhope, for example, obtained a royal grant of free warren on Midhope Moors in the late thirteenth century.

The medieval tenants of Hallamshire held their properties by one of two types of copyhold tenure. The old-established farms were recorded as hastler land, a term that was derived from a word that meant a spear. Hastler tenants were liable for military service if the lord required them to serve, and each year they elected a greave or grave as their representative at the manor court. The newer farmsteads that were laboriously cleared from the moors and woods were referred to as mattock land, from the tool that was used to stub out roots and unearth rocks. The Hallamshire manor court rolls that survive from 1277 record numerous clearances from the wastes, which the lord allowed upon payment of an entry fine and an agreed annual rent. These assarts, as they were called in the rolls, were typically small additions, from half-an-acre to 2 acres in extent, but some were even smaller.

In 1283, near the top of Hawkesworth Chase, Adam Hawkesworth paid a 2s.6d. entry fine and 3d. per annum rent for half-an-acre at Thornsett. The following year he paid to take in an extra one-eighth of an acre. In this way a new farm was created on the edge of the moors and a local surname came into being. The Hawkesworths were still farming at Thornsett three centuries later and Brian Hawkesworth farms there today. Elsewhere in the chapelry of Bradfield the farmers of the hamlets grew their oats in communal townfields that were divided into strips. Fourteenth-century documents record the townfields of Stannington, Ughill and Worrall and later records tell of a similar system of land division at Brightholmlee, Dungworth, Midhope, Onesacre and Wigtwizzle (where 120 strips in seven different parts of the townfield survived until the mid-eighteenth century). The same pattern is discernible from the records of many other townships and hamlets around the edges of the Peak District moors. At Roughbirchworth and, to a lesser extent, at Thurlstone, within the ancient parish of Penistone, the boundaries between blocks of strips are preserved by long, curving walls that were erected in the seventeenth century when the townfields were enclosed by agreement.

Wharncliffe Chase

The rugged escarpment of Wharncliffe Crags rises abruptly above the River Don on the north-eastern border of Hallamshire. Its name means the 'quern

cliff', for beehive-shaped hand querns for milling corn were fashioned here
out of millstone grit during the Roman period by native craftsmen, some of
whose dwellings have been identified from the remains of their foundations
nearby. Wharncliffe occupied the rough terrain on the western edge of
the lordship of Wortley and from 1252 it was used as a hunting chase. Sir
Thomas Wortley (c.1440–1514) rose to fame as a trusted 'knight of the king's
body' and he prospered as Sheriff of Yorkshire, Steward of Hallamshire and
steward of the estates of Fountains Abbey and Monk Bretton Priory.

His fondness for hunting led him to create a deer park by Wortley Hall and,
in 1510, a hunting lodge on the summit of Wharncliffe Crags. An inscription
commemorating this event is incorporated within the present building on
the old site. When Sir Richard Wortley inherited the family estates in 1583
he soon set about rebuilding Wortley Hall and enlarging his deer park there,
but when he extended Wharncliffe Chase and enclosed a New Park within
it, he met with fierce resistance from the leading minor gentry and yeoman
families of neighbouring Hallamshire, some of whom were the officers of
the Earl of Shrewsbury at Sheffield Castle and the Manor Lodge. The vicar
of Ecclesfield told the Court of Chancery in 1594 that a great part of the pale
of Wortley Park had been broken in pieces and pulled down in the night time
and that on several occasions the wall of Wharncliffe Chase had been 'pulled
down and overthrown' and the deer removed. He had also heard that:

> there weare little powles or sticks put upp in dyvers places within the
> Lordshipp of Wortley in the night season in forme of gallowes, and
> deeres fleshe hanged thereuppon … [and] that there was a deares head
> sett upp in the portche of the Chappell att Wortley and a slanderous
> Libel fixed or sewed therunto.

The vicar, too, had been the victim of the violent behaviour of the twenty-
seven men named in the charge. They had killed his tithe lambs and had
insulted him by the ritual disfigurement of his horse and mare. Others:

> had their horse tayles cutt and their fettlocks pared and shorne in the
> night tyme, and others theire flax mowen downe in the night beeinge
> but half ripe, and their geese necks writhen and killed and laid together
> beefore theire dores, and others had theire sheepe barrs cutt in peeces
> in the nighte, and another had his ram or tupp taken owte of his sheepe
> fowld and killed in the night tyme and the head and genitalls cutt of and

set uppon a maypole with a lewd and fylthy libell fixed to the same and others have had theire stone walles overthrowen and others theire dogges and swyne killed.

Yet the men who committed these outrages were not punished. They seem to have been retaliating against the wrongdoings of Sir Richard Wortley and his circle and to have been confident of the protection of the Earl of Shrewsbury. Sir Richard's overmighty bearing and actions were satirised in a popular ballad, *The Dragon of Wantley*, and a natural cleft in the crags near Wharncliffe Lodge acquired the name of 'The Dragon's Den'. When George Blount of More Hall in the valley below Wharncliffe Crags, on the other side of the River Don, won a court case concerning Sir Richard Wortley's collection of the tithes of Penistone, he was acclaimed as the 'More of More Hall' who slew the dragon with a mortal kick up the backside.

'The Dragon's Den', Wharncliffe Crags. This natural cleft in the crags near Wharncliffe Lodge acquired its nickname from the satirical ballad *The Dragon of Wantley*, which ridiculed Sir Richard Wortley and his ancestors for their ruthless actions: 'All sorts of cattle this dragon did eat,/ Some say he ate up trees,/ And that the forests sure he would/ Devour up by degrees:/ For houses and churches were to him geese and turkeys;/ He ate all, and left none behind,/ But some stones, dear Jack, that he could not crack,/ Which on the hills you will find.'

The northern moors

The boundary between the Norman lordship of Hallamshire and the Honour of Pontefract was formed by the Little Don River, beyond which rose the great ridge that bore the Celtic name *Pen*. This gave its name to Penistone, a parish of 22,773 acres divided into eight townships. The moors belonging to the westerly townships of Langsett and Thurlstone extended as far as the county boundary with Cheshire at Saltersbrook. In a particularly bleak spot, the Lords of Thurlstone had a vaccary that was recorded in the early fourteenth century at Windleden, the 'wind-swept

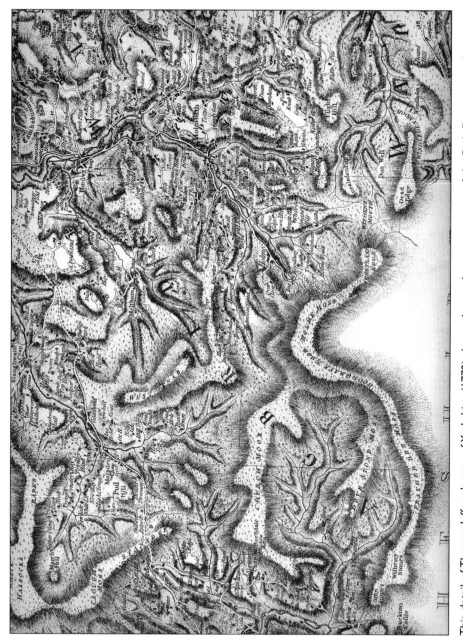

This detail of Thomas Jeffreys's map of Yorkshire (1772) shows the north-western moors of the Peak District, stretching from Saddleworth and Marsden to Meltham and the Graveship of Holme. They contain some of the bleakest scenery in England.

hill overlooking the valley'. Langsett township took its name from the long side of the *Pen* or great ridge that stretched from Hartcliff to Green Moor, but for much of the Middle Ages Langside or Langsett was known by the alternative name of Penisale, the 'nook of land on the edge of the estate' that was centred on Penistone. In the thirteenth century Penisale even had a short-lived Tuesday market and an annual three-day fair in June.

A case brought before the Court of Star Chamber in 1524 reveals the rivalry that existed between neighbouring lordships and the trouble that could occur when moorland boundaries were not well-defined on the ground. Complaints were made at the Thurlstone manor court that Holmfirth men, 'having recently taken in their own common', were driving cattle to graze on commons that belonged to Thurlstone. It was decided that local farmers should take turns to watch for these activities and drive the Holmfirth cattle away. But when Robert Mokeston was on duty he was attacked by three Holmfirth men who dragged him by the arm, knocked him to the ground, threw him into the river and almost kicked him to death. Edward Marsden saw this happen and came to Mokeston's help, but the pair were taken to the bailiff's house at Holmfirth, then escorted by 100 men to Sandal Castle, the administrative centre of the huge manor of Wakefield, of which Holmfirth formed part and whose lord, Sir Richard Tempest, was a bitter rival of Sir Henry Saville, the Lord of Thurlstone. When representatives from Thurlstone arrived at Sandal, they found that Mokeston had died. Tempest agreed to a trial at the next York Assizes, but when the Thurlstoners returned home, he announced a Not Guilty verdict. We do not know the final outcome of this case.

Beyond the north-western boundary of Penistone parish, the Graveship of Holme formed one of the twelve sub-divisions of the huge medieval manor of Wakefield. The officer responsible for each of these sub-divisions was known as the grave or greave. He was elected annually from amongst the tenants of the old-established farms and the office was held in an established rotation. The Graveship of Holme was recorded as 'Holnefrith' in 1274, the earliest surviving manor court roll, and not long afterwards as the 'Forresta de Holme, alias Holmfirthes', so it is clear that the name Holmfirth was applied originally to the whole graveship. Centuries later, Holmfirth became the more specific name of the industrial settlement that grew up in the valley bottom around the manorial corn and fulling mills. The 'forester of Holme' was recorded in the Wakefield manor court rolls from time-to-time until at least 1350. Throughout the Middle Ages the entire graveship was tenanted by copyholders, that is by people who kept a copy of the tenancy agreement that was entered in the manor court rolls, the earliest freehold properties date from late Elizabethan times. No large buildings of a military, domestic or public nature were erected within the medieval graveship, though a small chapel-of-ease was eventually built near the corn and fulling mills.

The careful control of grazing within the graveship is illustrated from the court roll of 1284 when John of Scholes was fined a shilling 'for taking into the trees two beasts more than he ought to forage', and in 1350 when the 'pannage of Holmefirth this year as presented by the forester there' amounted to 18d. and payments for 'summer agistment there' came to 12d. The court rolls also provide clues to the management of the local woods. For instance, in 1352 Matthew de Romesden was fined a shilling for cutting holly, presumably for winter fodder for his sheep, and in 1339 Adam del Grene was fined six shillings after his sheep had nibbled the lord's holly trees. In the same year, twenty-one men and women were each fined 8d. for nutting, and in 1352 Margery del Milne was fined 6d. for felling trees and 3s.4d. for selling six 'crokkes', that is crucks for building. The surviving cruck-framed buildings within the Graveship of Holme have not been dated by dendrochronology, but the earliest amongst those in Hallamshire are barns at Hall Broom Farm, Dungworth and Ughill Manor that have been dated to 1495–6 and 1504, respectively. This tradition of timber-framed building continued on the moorland edges well into the seventeenth century.

The 'long valley' of the river Etherow, forming the north-western 'panhandle' of Cheshire, was recorded as Longdendale in Domesday Book but is now usually known as the Woodhead Valley. This lordship lay immediately north of the Forest of the Peak, whose northern ward was also known as Longdendale. Much of the valley is now occupied by Manchester reservoirs. Longdendale was a separate medieval lordship between the River Thame and the upper portion of the valley of the River Etherow that stretched up the moors beyond Crowden to Saltersbrook and over the bogs of Featherbed Moss. The administrative centre of the medieval lordship was in the small borough of Tintwistle. From 1357 to 1374 the lordship of Longdendale was one of the many possessions of the Black Prince. A survey or extent of 1360 records a chase for red and fallow deer, a mill at Tintwistle, a fishery, a few smiths at work in their forges, payments for the pasturing of cattle, and fines for 'ploughing in lenten time'.

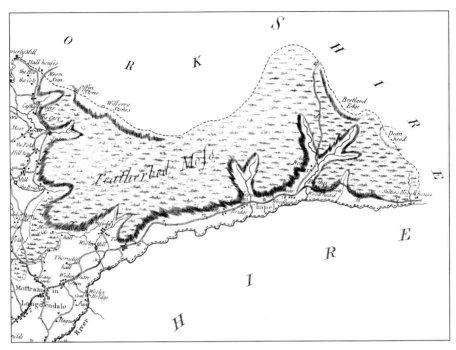

A detail of Burdett's map of Cheshire (1777), showing the ancient saltway (by then a turnpike road) along the Longdendale Valley, and the huge expanse of the boggy moors known as Featherbed Moss rising above.

Finally, the bleak moors and mosses at the north-western edge of the Peak District were divided between the two small manors, townships and chapelries of Meltham and Marsden at the western limit of the Honour of Pontefract, and Saddleworth, which lay within the West Riding although it was a chapelry of the Lancashire parish of Rochdale. These included some of the highest and wettest mosses in the Peak District: West Nab, Wessenden Head Moss, Black Hill and Holme Moss. The Saddleworth Firth that was recorded occasionally between 1316 and 1553 may have been in the Quick Mere quarter of the chapelry, but little is known about its history.

The thirteenth century was a period of 'high farming' when both lay and ecclesiastical lords employed stewards to manage their estates directly rather than lease them to tenants. Prices for agricultural produce were high and the demand for wool from the clothiers of Flanders and Italy was buoyant. But a series of devastating cattle plagues, sheep murrains and harvest failures between 1315 and 1322 caused the rural economy to contract long before the

Black Death of 1348–49. A comparison of the taxes paid to Pope Nicholas in 1291 and those paid in the 'Inquisition of the Ninth' of 1341 reveals a considerable decline. In most townships along the moorland edges the assessment for 1341 was much lower than the previous one. For example, Penistone's fell from £53.6s.8d. to £20 and much land lay waste. Likewise, in 1332 the *inquisition post mortem* of Thomas de Furnival, lord of Hallamshire, noted that 240 acres of arable in Sheffield were uncultivated and that the rents from grazing had declined from £6 to £1.16s.8d. per annum. Then came the huge mortalities caused by the Black Death.

We have hardly any information as to what happened to the moorland communities of the Peak District when this pestilence raged, but at Macclesfield in 1348–49 no rents were gathered for forty-six holdings. Nevertheless, by 1355 only six of these farms were still unlet. The farms that were abandoned were mostly re-occupied in the later Middle Ages, though the least desirable, such as Lawrence Field above Padley Gorge, were never reclaimed. In the changed conditions great landlords found themselves short of a ready supply of labour and so, faced by demands for higher wages, they abandoned pastoral farming and leased their estates to tenants. The monastic landowners too were forced to adopt this new policy.

Monastic granges

The monks and canons who were grateful recipients of generous gifts of moorland from feudal lords used lay brothers and day labourers to work their estates from granges, which were in essence superior farmsteads that usually had a chapel attached. Monastic granges were of great importance in the development of remote parts of the Peak District, both on the higher reaches of the limestone plateau and on the surrounding gritstones. In most cases these granges were established on new or abandoned sites. The Cistercians, who owned about half the granges in the Peak District, from Saddleworth in the north to Morridge in the south, were particularly keen to exploit isolated territory and they had a reputation for driving away their neighbours.

Medieval granges are poorly documented and the buildings that have not been replaced by later structures survive only as foundations or as earthworks. Studies of crowberry pollen have shown that the southern Pennine moors enjoyed a warm period in the twelfth and early thirteenth centuries and that the next 200 years were relatively dry. This benign climate encouraged the monasteries to exploit their summer pastures high on the moors. A typical sheep grange, known in the records as a bercary, had a flock of 200–300 and a typical vaccary had twenty to eighty head of cattle. Although the herds of cattle were more reliant on enclosed pastures than were the sheep, they too grazed on the open moors. The dominance of sheep in the moorland landscape was a later development.

The monasteries themselves lay well beyond the Peak District. For example, the Cistercian abbey at Merevale (Warwickshire) received an estate near Chinley that is still known as Monk's Meadows and a house and land at Fairfield, together with a large area of good-quality pasture to the north-east of Buxton. In the late twelfth century William, the son of John, Lord of Penistone, provided Kirkstead Abbey, a Cistercian house in Lincolnshire, with moorland next to the grange that they had already established at Penisale. Perhaps the name of Sheephouse Farm in Langsett township

points to a likely candidate for the site? In the 1230s the abbey received permission to move sixty cattle from their grange at Thundercliffe, 12 miles to the east of Penisale, onto the common pastures of Langsett township, presumably for summer grazing. The most substantial gift was that made by King Henry II in or about 1157 to the Cistercian abbey of Basingwerk (Clwyd) of the manor and church of Glossop. The eastern boundary of this manor was marked by the Lady Cross, whose base still stands on the skyline high above Saltersbrook, and by Devil's Dyke, which separated Charlesworth township from the Hopedale ward of the Forest of the Peak. This ditch is 7–10 metres wide and 2–3 metres deep and it now forms part of the

Devil's Dyke, near Bleaklow, was the ancient boundary of the Cistercian abbey of Basingwerk's manor of Glossop within the Forest of the Peak. It followed the watershed and was known in 1627 as Shelf Dyke. The Devil's Dyke appears to be a later name, first recorded in 1840. Its course is now followed by the Pennine Way.

Shillito Cross is one of three medieval crosses that appear to mark the moorland boundaries of the estate granted by the Lord of Barlow to the Cistercian monks of Louth Park Abbey.

Pennine Way. In the later Middle Ages the Abbots of Basingwerk claimed that their estate lay outside the jurisdiction of the encircling Forest of the Peak.

In the twelfth and thirteenth centuries the Cistercian monks of Louth Park Abbey (Lincolnshire) were granted estates in Barlow and neighbouring townships, which extended up on to the eastern moors. These monks seem to have been responsible for the erection of Whibbersley Cross in Leash Fen, together with a tall cross in Shillito Wood and a similar cross at a high point on Fox Lane, in order to mark their boundaries. They built their grange on the edge of the moors, on or near the site of the seventeenth-century farmhouse known still as Barlow Grange (the 'Barley Grange' that was recorded in 1306), which stands on the skyline when viewed from the valley below. They also built a house a few hundred yards to the south at Birley, which took its name from a cattle byre. The other nearby names – Grange Lumb, Grange Hill, Grange House – are all derived from Barlow Grange.

When the Breton lord of the manor, Hascoit Muscard, granted Birley to the monks in the twelfth century, the bounds of the property extended from Oxton Rakes 'to the shepherd's house of Robert Musard, thence to the hawthorn, from the hawthorn to the oak, and from the oak to the hollywell and from the hollywell all the cultivated land as far as the moor'. We get a vivid sense of a wild landscape with few features that could be used as boundary markers. Some time in the twelfth century Walter de Abetoft and Robert his son granted to Louth Park Abbey the right to erect two forges or hearths in the woods and a forge in the monks' courtyard at the grange. A further grant in 1314 allowed the monks to forge and smelt iron there, using fuel and iron ore from Barlow woods.

Several Peak District granges were established on the Staffordshire Moorlands. In 1214 Earl Ranulf founded Dieulacres Abbey for the Cistercian order and donated the manor of Leek. The monks soon built granges in Leek and Lowe, then at Birchall, and later at Westwood, Heaton, Leekfrith and Tittesworth. In 1490 they owned seventeen cows and a bull, 118 steers, heifers and stirks, and seventy-two oxen and cows at Swythamley in Heaton, where they had pastures in the 'forest' at Leekfrith, including The Roaches. They also had ten draught oxen at Swythamley. By the 1530s the granges at Birchall and Westwood were leased to the Brereton family of Westwood.

The large parish of Leek contained other Cistercian granges at Bradnop and Onecote on the southern end of Morridge. Pasture rights on Morridge were included in Henry de Audley's endowment of Hulton Abbey in 1223, but when a grange was established at Mixon in Onecote a dispute with the monks of Dieulacres Abbey occurred. An agreement was reached in 1237 whereby the abbey retained pasture rights on Morridge for pigs 'without number', and in the summer for 200 dry cattle. By 1343 Hulton Abbey also had a grange in the north part of Bradnop township, which they let to William Gonne, along with pasture rights on Morridge for all animals except goats (which were notoriously destructive). The Cistercians of Croxden Abbey, near Uttoxeter, also had a grange at Onecote by 1223. A little later, other local benefactors donated further land to Dieulacres Abbey, for example in Rudyard manor, where the connection is commemorated by the minor place-names Abbey Farm, Abbey Green and Abbey Wood. Granges were also established in the upper part of the Meer Brook at Roche, Westwood and Foker (the 'foul marsh'). At that time, sheep farming was of prime importance in this locality, but in the late fifteenth century the granges were geared towards the rearing of cattle. By King Henry VIII's reign, most of them were leased to neighbouring landowners.

A preaching order of canons, founded at Prémontré in northern France and modelled on the Cistercians, built granges in the Upper Derwent Valley and along the eastern edge of the Peak District moors. At the end of the twelfth century King John granted the Premonstratensian canons of Welbeck Abbey 'the pasture of Crookhill, the woods of Ashop up to Lockerbrook and from Lockerbrook up the valley of the Derwent and ascending up to Derwenthead' within the royal Forest of the Peak. The grange that they founded at Crookhill Farm had a horse stud for twenty horses and twenty mares, a vegetable garden and an orchard, and 50 acres of pasture for eighty

Crook Hill. A modern farm occupies the site of the medieval grange that belonged to the Premonstratensian canons of Welbeck Abbey. King John granted the canons an extensive moorland estate in the Upper Derwent Valley, where they were allowed to keep a horse stud and to graze eighty cattle. Upon the dissolution of the monasteries, the estate was purchased by the Cavendish family. William Senior's survey of 1627 showed that it covered 447 acres, including 165 acres in 'The great pasture'. Crook is a word that was used in prehistoric times to mean a hill.

cattle. The grange that they established in the 1250s at One Man's House, a former hermitage on the east bank of the Derwent, had extensive pasture rights within the chapelry of Bradfield.

In the thirteenth century the canons built a chapel at Derwent, a corn mill, a bridge on the highway from Sheffield to Hope, and reputedly two more chapels, one near Birchinlee and the other on the track from Hope to Glossop, although neither of these has been dated definitely to the Middle Ages. Pottery and documentary evidence suggest that by the end of the thirteenth century most of the farmsteads in the Upper Derwent Valley belonged to Welbeck abbey. The canons were probably also responsible for introducing the smelting of lead with charcoal fuel in the valley bottom, where Bill Bevan has discovered numerous charcoal platforms and hearths and three smelting boles.

Settlements in the Upper Derwent Valley that were definitely founded in the Middle Ages include Alport, Crookhill, Derwent hamlet, Grimbocar, Nether Ashop, One Man's House, Ronksley, Rowlee, Shireowlers, Tinker's House and Westend, each of them about half-a-mile apart. Large collections of potsherds dating from medieval and later times have been found scattered around the sites of the farmsteads at One Man's House, Ronksley, Shireowlers, Tinker's House and Nether Ashop, and Crown rentals for Derwent and Hope Woodlands between 1339 and 1413 name farms at Alport, Grimbocar, Ronksley, Rowlee and Westend. Others that were possibly medieval, but which are not recorded until later, include Ashop, Bamford House, Birchinlee, Blacklowe, Dovestone Clough, Dryclough, Grainfoot, Hollin Clough, Lockerbrook, Parkinfield, Underbank and Welkers Farm. Nearly all of them were placed on the sides of the valley, just below the moors. In the later Middle Ages these properties were leased to tenants, who sub-let them to peasant farmers, and at the dissolution of the monasteries they were bought by the Earl of Shrewsbury of Sheffield Castle or by Sir William Cavendish of Chatsworth.

The Premonstratensian canons of Beauchief Abbey owned at least seven granges on the moors or the adjoining coal-measure sandstones. The largest one was sited on the eastern edge of Beeley Moor, where a farmhouse still bears the name of Harewood Grange. The original grant by Warner or Warin of Beeley allowed pasture on the moors there for 100 oxen and cows, twenty horses with their young and 100 sheep. Further grants by his descendants and by neighbouring landowners extended the grazing area to the western side of Beeley Moor and into the parish of Ashover and the chapelry of Walton. Some of the small boundary stones that can be found on these moors probably date from this era. On Christmas Eve 1335 Thomas of Beeley confirmed the grants of land, tenements, dues and services made by his ancestors and offered a new gift, 'for the sake of his soul and of that of his wife

Lady Cross, Big Moor. This thirteenth-century cross marked the limit of the moorland estate that was granted to the Premonstratensian canons of Beauchief Abbey. In later times it acted as a manorial boundary. This side is inscribed 'M B', signifying the manor of Baslow. The cross also served as a waymarker on the route over the moors from the Hope Valley to Sheffield.

Cecily', of common of pasture for eighty she-goats and their young under one year, and of heather, turf, bracken and quarry stone for all the canons' needs, 'at Harewood grange below the common pasture at Beeley'.

The lands of another Beauchief Abbey grange at Strawberry Lee, west of Totley and just in sight from the abbey, can be identified as an extensive green area surrounded by moorland on all sides. A farmhouse stood on this site until 1936, but today only some ruined walls remain. In the thirteenth century the canons received grants of common pasture for goats and other animals, which eventually extended over Hathersage and Padley Moors. The stump of the Lady Cross, marking the boundary of the canons' possessions, survives in its original position over a mile away from the grange.

A third grange, at Fulwood across the border in Hallamshire, was recorded in a mid-thirteenth-century charter in the Beauchief Abbey cartulary as a grant from Thomas de Furnival, Lord of Hallamshire. It presumably occupied the site of the present Fulwood Grange Farm a few hundred yards from Fulwood Booth. The canons were given 'sufficient common pasture ... for all their animals, except goats' and common rights, including 'quarries, turbaries, branches and bracken for roofing their houses' and sufficient land from the waste 'for mending and extending their ditches'.

Other religious organisations benefited in different ways. For example, the Lovetots donated two-thirds of the tithes of Hallamshire to the Benedictine abbey of St Wandrille, which was sited a few miles away from their native village in Normandy, and the remaining third was given to the Augustinian priory they founded at Worksop. By contrast, the Knights of the Hospital of St John of Jerusalem gathered many small donations from ordinary farmers. In the chapelry of Bradfield, for example, they held six properties in Ughill and another six in Waldershelf, which they administered from their preceptory at Newland, near Halifax. Their custom of marking their properties with crosses to show that they were not obliged to pay tithes was continued by later owners. Platts Farm, near Ughill, still displays such crosses in its corbels.

Townships and hamlets

The terms 'moor' and 'common' were interchangeable right through to the era of parliamentary enclosure in the late eighteenth and early nineteenth centuries. 'Moor' was used regularly to denote a common pasture on the edge of a town or village, regardless of its size and appearance. Sheffield retains the names of Crookesmoor and Shalesmoor, and what is now a central

Broomhead Dyke. This deep ditch was dug to mark the medieval boundary of the hamlet of Wigtwizzle long before the wall was built alongside it in the early nineteenth century.

shopping street is known simply as The Moor. Other moors that nowadays have a general name, such as the Big Moor or the Eastern Moors, were once known more precisely by the names of the townships, meres or hamlets to which particular stretches belonged. The chapelry of Saddleworth was divided into four quarters, or meres: Lordsmere, Friarmere, Shawmere and Quickmere, and in the parish of Penistone the western part of Thurlstone township was known as Thurlstone Mere. The word 'mere' meant a boundary and, by extension, it came to describe the adjacent district.

The term 'hamlet' was used not just in its present sense of a few farmsteads and cottages but for a sub-division of a township. The origins of these hamlets are unknown but some were recorded in Domesday Book. Their ancient boundaries were sometimes marked on the first edition of the 6-inch Ordnance Survey map during the reign of Queen Victoria, nearly 800 years later. Some hamlets had their own townfields, divided into strips for the communal cultivation of oats and sometimes other cereals, with pastures and moorland wastes beyond, and occasionally with a communal wood. For example, the hamlet of Longley within the Graveship of Holme had its own townfields and common and Longleyhirst ('the wood of Longley'). Decisions about day-to-day farming activities were taken at the local level of the hamlet and ratified later at the manorial court.

The growth of the national population between the twelfth and the early fourteenth centuries brought renewed pressure to create farmsteads and hamlets by clearing land from the edges of the moors. Oats were grown or livestock were reared in small, irregular-shaped fields that were recorded as assarts in the manor court rolls. The great feudal lords were pleased to increase their revenues by encouraging these clearances and by charging whatever rents the market would bear. For example, the Wakefield manor court rolls record that in 1309 William, son of Thomas of Hallamshire, paid a shilling entry fine and an annual rent of 6d. to take an acre of new land from the waste in Hepworth 'in front of his door'. Another entry for the Graveship of Holme in 1332 noted that Henry Wade had paid the lord a two shillings entry fine 'for licence to take an acre of land from the lord's waste in Haddes in Holme to be held by him and his heirs rendering per annum 4d new rent'. This assart can be identified with the headland known as Hade Edge, which was first recorded six years earlier, high above Wooldale.

This medieval wall marked the boundary of a clearing in the present Longshaw Estate on the opposite side of Padley Gorge to Lawrence Field. It probably dates from the late twelfth or thirteenth centuries when people were desperate for land. These assarts, as they were known, were often abandoned after the Black Death had reduced the population drastically.

Further south, in 1440–41, Edward of Ryles and Agnes, his wife, and Richard, his son, were licensed by the lord of Hallamshire to 'pluck up by the roots and clear away, in all lands that could be ploughed, thorns brambles and thicket' at what is now Rails Farm, near Stannington, high above the Rivelin Valley. The common vernacular terms for these assarts were stubbing or intake (usually pronounced intack) and in the West Riding the dialect word royd was often used with the personal name of the man or woman who had made the clearing. Only a few royd names are found within Hallamshire, but the term was very popular further north. This process of establishing new farms on the moorland edges continued right up to the Black Death.

The boundaries of these new farmsteads were marked by ditches and banks that were often surmounted by hedges. The minor place-name *hey* meant a hedged enclosure. But in some instances, such as at Lawrence Field, low stone walls were constructed. These walls had a very different appearance from the present drystone walls that cover so much of the Peak District landscape, for they were simply a rough series of boulders placed upright, known to archaeologists as 'orthostats'. Few of them survive but they were perhaps more common than the sparse medieval records suggest. In Hallamshire, for instance, a document that can be dated to before 1290 refers to 'le rie croft on the west side of Uggil, as surrounded by a stone wall … and all his part of that moor which lay between the old dike and the new dike … next the cross of Richard'.

The ditches and banks that were used as moorland boundaries to divide the sheepwalks and outpastures of the various hamlets or townships, or of individual farms, show how local communities took care to organise their moorland resources for the benefit of all. A long ditch across Cartledge Stones Ridge, high on the Bradfield Moors, which separated the lord of Hallamshire's pastures at Howden from the commons that belonged to Cowell and Wigtwizzle hamlets, now marks the boundary of the National Trust's High Peak Estate. Some of these moorland ditches also served as drains.

Many of the names of these farmsteads and hamlets on the edges of the moors were used as surnames by the families who lived in them during the thirteenth and fourteenth centuries. These scattered settlements produced a much higher proportion of surnames that were derived from minor place-names than did other parts of England where families lived in villages. Most of these distinctive surnames remained characteristic of their native districts over the succeeding centuries. Littlewood, for instance, retains a strong presence in the Graveship of Holme, where it was derived from a clearance in the little wood of Cartworth. A William de Lyttlewode and a Geppe de Lyttlewode were recorded there in the earliest surviving court roll of the manor of Wakefield in 1274. Other surnames that were derived from farmsteads in the graveship include Broadhead, Brownhill, Hinchcliffe and Ramsden, all of which were recorded in the years leading up to the Black Death, and Oxley, which first appeared in a court roll for 1374. Biltcliff, Bullas, Reaney and Swinden were surnames that were derived from isolated farmsteads in the moorland townships of Penistone parish, while Broomhead, Dungworth and Moorwood emerged in the neighbouring chapelry of Bradfield.

The Ronksleys, who became established in Bradfield during the late Middle Ages, took their name from Ronksley Farm on the right bank of the River Derwent. John de Ronkeslai was recorded there in 1366, and in 1415 Barten de Ronkysley became the tenant of 'the Mickle Holden and Holden Hedes pastures late in the possession of Thomas de Ronksley'. In the lay subsidy return of 1546, however, the farm was tenanted by Thomas Barbur.

The Staffordshire moorlands too had their characteristic surnames, such as Brunt from Brund, Fernihough from a farmstead in Endon township in the parish of Leek, and Greatbach from Gradbach Farm on the Cheshire border. A Henry Gratebache was recorded in the Forest of Alstonefield in 1374. In the High Peak, surnames sprang from small places such as Derwent, Froggatt, Offerton or Ollerenshaw, or from villages on the fringes of the moors, such as Buxton, Charlesworth, Glossop, Hadfield and Padley. And on the northern border of the Peak District, Marsden became one of the most prolific surnames of all.

Other farms on the edge of the Pennines, however, take their names from the men who first cleared the land in the thirteenth or fourteenth centuries. High above the Ewden Valley a farm known as Snell House appears to be a typical nineteenth-century smallholding at the highest point of cultivation, yet the documentary evidence tells us that this land has been farmed for over six-and-a-half centuries. The book of customary fines of the lordship of Hallamshire records that in 1342 Elias Snel 'gave 6d. for licence to hold one plot of land in Westmondhalgh by the gift of Hugh de Whitley'. Westmondhalgh was the ancient name of one of the four townships or bierlows in the soke of Bradfield within the manor of Sheffield, and White Lee Farm lies just a quarter-of-a-mile away, so there is no doubting the identification. In the Bradfield poll tax returns of 1379 a William Snell paid the basic rate of 4d. The family then disappeared from local records, but the name of their moorland farm survived.

Saltways

Although the moors presented formidable difficulties to travellers in the winter months, they were nevertheless crossed by well-trodden tracks that followed the most convenient routes. A distinctive group of traders carried salt from the Cheshire 'wiches' at Northwich, Middlewich and Nantwich to the medieval market towns of Yorkshire, Derbyshire and Nottinghamshire. Salt was a precious commodity, for it was used to preserve food as well as to flavour it. Minor place-names enable us to map the routes taken by the salters, names such as Salterway, Salter Hill or Salter Ford. Other traders too used these tracks, but the salters were the most prominent. Domesday Book provides hints of how vigorous the trade was in the late eleventh century, when fifteen boilings of a pan were needed to make a packhorse load of salt. Tolls were levied at the rate of four pence for every load drawn by four or more oxen, two pence for a load led by two oxen, two pence for a packhorse load, and a farthing for a load carried on a man's back. The local carriers were allowed cheaper rates. The long-distance journeys across the High Peak would have been too difficult for a man to have carried a pack efficiently or for wheeled vehicles to have negotiated the steep hills, so salt was almost certainly taken by packhorses on a round trip of four to six days.

The most important medieval tracks, above the level of the ubiquitous lanes, were known either by the Anglo-Saxon word which became 'way' or by the Viking word which developed into 'gate'. Thus, the routes from outlying farmsteads to the parish church were known either as Church Ways or Kirk Gates. The most northerly of the salt tracks across the Peak District moors crossed the Hull Brook in the chapelry of Saddleworth at Salterhebble, the 'salters' bridge'. Further south an important salters' route from Northwich followed the Saltersway to Altrincham and went past the field- or farm-name Salters Hey on the approach to Stockport before climbing the Longdendale Valley towards the Yorkshire market towns of Rotherham, Barnsley, Doncaster and Wakefield. The long, narrow extension of the county of Cheshire that was created to take in the Longdendale Valley demonstrates the crucial importance of this route in the Anglo-Saxon period, and probably long before.

Having crossed Saltersbrook, the boundary stream that separated Cheshire from Yorkshire at the eastern end of the valley, the salters soon parted ways. Some veered left towards Wakefield along the track that was recorded variously as Salterway or Saltergate and which delineated part of the boundary between the Graveship of Holme and the township of Thurlstone.

Those who kept straight on and climbed up to the Lady Cross headed for Rotherham via Salter Hill, Salter Close, Psalter Field and Psalter Lane, or towards Barnsley and Doncaster past Salter Croft, another Saltersbrook, and Saltergate at Scawsby.

The routes from the salt works at Middlewich into Derbyshire are well-marked by appropriate names, starting with the crossing of the River Dane at Saltersford, which was replaced by a stone bridge in 1331. Siddington was then approached along Salters Lane where the Middlewich men may have been joined on their way to Macclesfield by salters coming from Northwich. So far the way had been level going, but beyond Macclesfield the steep climbs began. The most northerly of the three hill routes across the Peak District followed the course of the present road towards Whaley Bridge and crossed the River Goyt at Heybottom Bridge, before continuing to Chapel-en-le-Frith and down the Winnats Pass to Castleton. The salters may have rested overnight at Hope, for here was a Salter Barn and in 1688 a Salter Furlong just to the south of the village. Fields with salter names attached to them seem to have provided overnight grazing stops for the horses. The next day the packhorses were led along Saltergate Lane near Bamford and up the steep escarpment at Stanedge, where they entered Hallamshire. Sheffield was approached via Psalter Lane, which in 1485 was recorded as Salter Lane.

The medieval saltway climbed from Saltersbrook to its highest point at the Lady Cross, a boundary stone erected by the Cistercian monks of Basingwerk Abbey to mark the eastern limit of their manor of Glossop. The cross was recorded as a boundary point in 1290. The chamfered base is original, but the stone that serves as a shaft has been placed there in modern times. The highway was made into a turnpike road in 1741 and is still used as a moorland track.

An alternative route from Macclesfield avoided the steeper hills and headed for the Saltersford (which was recorded in 1452) near Goyt's Bridge and then up the Long Hill to Buxton. A third route, which was the most difficult line of all, approached Buxton across wild terrain, now marked at the summit by the Cat and Fiddle inn. On leaving Buxton the salters took a lane through Fairfield and across the Saltersford that was recorded in 1272 at the southern edge of Tideswell Townend. They may have rested at the three closes named Salter's Flatt, a few hundred yards to the south in Wormhill, before descending the Sir William Hill to Grindleford and crossing the Bar Brook at Salters Ford. The salters who were heading for Chesterfield climbed the escarpment beyond the River Derwent to Curbar Gap and crossed the eastern moors before entering the market town via Saltergate.

The most southerly of these ancient saltways can be traced from Congleton, which was conveniently near all three of the Cheshire wiches. When the townships of Leek and Onecote were indicted at the quarter sessions in 1749 for not repairing this 'great carriers' road ... chiefly used by packhorses who carry salt out of Cheshire into Derbyshire and Nottinghamshire and bring back malt into Cheshire', it was claimed that more than 100 horses loaded with salt used this road every week. We do not have comparable evidence for the use of the way in the Middle Ages, but there is no doubt that medieval salters too had used this route over Morridge to Warslow, Winster and the medieval bridge at Darley, and on to Saltergate in Chesterfield or down Salters Lane to Matlock.

The medieval ways and gates across the moors attracted other names too. The routes taken by burial parties from outlying districts to the parish church, such as those heading from the Graveship of Holme to Kirkburton or from Carlecotes to Penistone, acquired the description Corpse Way. The dialect word rakes, meaning a path, survives in Wreakes Lane (Dronfield) and Oxton Rakes (Barlow), the 'Oxrakes de Barley' of 1330 by which oxen were driven up on to the moorland pastures in summertime. The jaggers, who transported lead or coal by packhorse, are commemorated by the Jaggers' Lane that was recorded in 1408 in Heathylee township and by similar names elsewhere, such as Jaggers' Lane (Hathersage), Jaggers' Gate on the boundary of the Forest of the Peak between the Rivers Wye and Goyt, and others on the limestone at Ashover and Darley.

Communications were not restricted to packhorses for oxen-drawn, two-wheeled wains were a common sight. Domesday Book recorded an annual tribute of five wain loads of lead to the lord of the manor of Hope, and the

Hallamshire court rolls of 1446–7 noted 'the expense of 120 persons with 60 wains, and their draught-oxen, coming to do boon-work, and carrying limestone from Roche Abbey' to Sheffield Castle. The regular use of wains, and sometimes the more sturdy carts, is demonstrated by the survival of several medieval bridges across the Rivers Derwent and Wye that were broad enough to take wheeled vehicles, even before they were widened in later centuries. Fine examples survive at Bakewell, Cromford, Darley and Matlock. The narrower packhorse bridges were wooden structures until they were rebuilt in stone in the seventeenth and eighteenth centuries.

Moorland industries

Moorland men often supplemented their income by mining coal in shallow pits, smelting lead or bog iron, or making charcoal in the coppice woods. As many as 238 sub-circular platforms for the burning of charcoal have been identified in Bill Bevan's survey of the Upper Derwent Valley, some of them dating back to the thirteenth century. Lead was smelted on windy escarpments known as bole hills, such as those high above Barlow or at Crookesmoor, where they are commemorated by minor place-names, and Boler became a distinctive Derbyshire surname for someone who worked as a lead smelter. As we have seen at Yarncliff, the hewing of millstones for water-powered corn mills and windmills was a well-established occupation by the fifteenth century. Much further back in time, Wharncliffe got its name from 'the quern cliff' and on the Staffordshire Moorlands Quarnford too derived its name from the manufacture of the beehive-shaped querns that were used for hand milling in a previous era.

The greatest permanent influence on the moorland landscape, however, came from the cutting of peat for domestic and industrial fuel. The village of Flagg, which was recorded in Domesday Book, took its name from an Old Norse word meaning the 'place where turves were cut', so the custom was clearly an ancient one. Peat was dug in both the Dark Peak and parts of the White Peak throughout the Middle Ages and well into the modern era on a very large scale. Each moorland farmstead had its share of the local turbaries, to which they were linked by the holloways that can still be followed on the ground. Over the centuries the stripping away of the peat converted much of the heather moorland into the grassy pastures that sheep still graze today.

Chapter 4

'A waste and houling wilderness' 1550–1750

The nature of the moors

Tudor and Stuart people regarded the moors in very different ways from the Romantic writers and artists of the late eighteenth and nineteenth centuries, who saw them as places of beauty and spiritual calm. Early writers came up with adjectives such as awful, dismal, frightful, gloomy, hideous, horrible, inhospitable and unpleasing, while manorial stewards and surveyors dismissed the moors as 'waste' or as 'barren ground' of no economic value or aesthetic appeal. Their preference was for a tamed, productive landscape.

William Camden, the great Elizabethan antiquary, thought that The Roaches, north of Leek, formed 'a tract so very rugged, foul, and cold that the snows continue long undissolved'. Shortly afterwards, in 1611, the jury of a neighbouring manor court described Sheen as mostly 'cold, stony, barren ground', which during the winter was 'commonly so troubled with winds, frosts, and snow as cattle cannot endure to stay thereupon'. Further north, a contemporary visitor to Marsden found its 'rude mountains' were 'vast, stonie, moorish and barren' and the land was 'weet, sobbed and rotten'. This is a far cry from Spencer Hall's positive view of Hallamshire in *The Peak and the Plain* (1857): 'In all Britain are not to be found spots more primitive or romantic than some in that neighbourhood.'

Visitors to the Peak District from the south of England were particularly fearful of this wild terrain. When Daniel Defoe travelled from Chesterfield to Chatsworth in the early eighteenth century, he marvelled at the 'vast extended moor or waste, which, for 15 or 16 miles together due north, presents you with neither hedge, house or tree, but a waste and houling wilderness, over which when strangers travel, they are obliged to take guides, or it would be next to impossible not to lose their way'. He complained afterwards about 'this difficult desart country' and 'the comfortless, barren … endless moor'. When he eventually reached the High Peak, he thought it was 'the most desolate, wild, and abandoned country in all England'.

The very real dangers that threatened those who crossed the moors in wintertime are revealed by entries in the Penistone burial register: '10 March 1755 Wm Wordsworth Starv'd to Death on the Moors; 15 February 1763 Jos. Charlesworth from Burton lost in Snow; 6 March 1764 James Marsh starv'd in the Snow.' An earlier record in the Eyam burial register for 4 February 1692 noted that Elizabeth, the wife of John Trout, 'dyed upon the Moor near unto Sir William, a place so called, coming from Tideswell Market in a snow'. Likewise, the curate of the chapelry of Bradfield wrote in his burial register for 25 August 1718: 'Memorandum – a coffin put in the earth with Bones of a Person found upon the high Moors, thought to be Richard Stede.' Then on 31 December 1725 John Hobson of Dodworth Green, near Barnsley, recorded that Mr Baines, the parson of Barlow and schoolmaster of Dronfield, met his death in a great snowfall on Froggatt

Cut Gate. Thomas Jeffreys marked this route from Slippery Stones to Langsett as a Bridle Way on his map of Yorkshire (1772). John Derry, *Across the Derbyshire Moors* (1904), an account of twelve walks near Sheffield that was extended by G.H.B. Ward in 1934 and 1939, noted in the twenty-third edition (1946) that 'the street-wide ancient bridle way called Cut gate [was, within living memory] repaired annually by the employees of the Duke of Norfolk and Mr Thomasson, Grain Foot, Derwent, so that the Derwent woodland farmers could ride to Penistone market. It is doubtful, however, if the public authorities have spent a penny in repairing this moorland part of the bridle way since 1900.' Its ancient course down from the summit to Slippery Stones was marked by 'upright stakes at intervals'.

Moss while on his way to Grindleford Bridge. The following winter Hobson noted that Tuesday 13 December 1726 was 'such an ill day for frost, snow and wind, that severall people had like to have perished in comming over the moors from Woodhead, and some lost their lives in going from Sheffield to Heithersedge'.

The most grisly account of all is contained in the diary of Arthur Jessop of Lydgate, near Holmfirth, who on 11 May 1731 heard that:

Thomas Littlewood's Son who was lost of the 25 of March is found on Westnab. It is between 6 & 7 weeks since he was lost. The child was found yesterday the 10 in the afternoon a good way beyond the Westnab. Its head was eaten off and its skull left bare, its hands were gone and its arms as far as could be seen for its waistcoat sleeves appeared to be empty. It had its waistcoat on and cloth buttons but there were some ribs came out of its Breeches. Its Hose & Shoes and its feet & legs were not touched. They brought & wrapped it in a blanket to Meltorn [Meltham] Chapel.

This sounds like a similar misfortune to the one that befell the Lost Lad who was commemorated by the name of a prominent rock high above the Upper Derwent Valley.

The best contemporary description of the variety of vegetation on a Pennine moor in the Elizabethan period comes from much further north in the West Riding, where an intake or new enclosure on the edge of Rawdon Moor in the parish of Guiseley was the subject of a tithe dispute. Some of the disputants spoke of 'all the tufts or busshes of heath' that grew on the dry land, and that: 'immediatelye before the taking in and ploughing of the Intakk the moore parte of the ground … was fair and good Grene gyrs [grass] and swerth ground, yea twoo partes of yt yea three partes of yt was grene and swarth ground … and no heath growing upon it.' Before it was enclosed the intake was 'a verey good pasture ground for all maner of Cattell as horses mares kye [dairy cows] sheepe swyne and gees … part of yt was grene gyrs before yt was ploughed upp'.

Other witnesses maintained that 'although the place where the Intake is situate … is called Rawdon Moore yet namelye in the same Intake there nether was yet is any moorishe weet sobbed or rotten ground but is and always hayth bene a good and fair ground for gyrs [grass] and corne'. In explanation they said that 'it is a common usage of the same countrye to call their common pasture a moore althoughe there be lytell or noo morish ground in yt'. Thomas Lynley of Deane Grange, a 40-year old yeoman, mentioned 'one pece of bentishe grounde which is something wete in winter but in somer it is and longe haith bene fair and dry mete for gris or corne' and Michael Rawden, the farmer of the tithe of Rawdon Moor, spoke of the parts 'where leest ling or heath did grew' and 'some gresse pyles that grewed emongest the ling bent and brakens'.

Moorland farms

As the national population rose from the second quarter of the sixteenth century onwards, so the pressure on the moorland edges increased. Although no new moorland villages were created, hamlets and isolated farmsteads reappeared in the landscape. On the Staffordshire Moorlands, for example, the older farms of over 100 acres, which occupy the best land in the valleys

The ruins of Bamford House. Each of the scattered farms in the Upper Derwent Valley had its own fields, cattle pastures, sheepwalks and turbaries, where peat was cut for fuel. Deep holloways leading up to the moors intersect at this point.

and on the hillsides, can be distinguished from the small farms of under 20 acres that were created on the higher ground from Elizabethan times onwards. On the other side of the Peak District in 1551, seven tenants of the Graveship of Holme were licensed by the manor court to rent intakes 'of land lately encroached from the lord's waste' that varied in size from half a rood to 7 acres. Their activities were replicated in all the townships around the Peak District moors.

The inhabitants of these moorland fringes framed their houses with crucks and roofed them with thatch, turf or bracken. Dendrochronological analysis (a computerised form of tree-ring dating) has placed the majority of the surviving cruck-framed moorland farmhouses, cottages and barns in the sixteenth and early seventeenth centuries. Most dwellings were small structures with just a single fireplace. A passage between the front and rear entrances ran behind the hearth and separated the living and sleeping quarters from the service end. This hearth-passage type of vernacular housing seems to have been a natural development from the medieval longhouse, once the livestock had been moved elsewhere and the lower end of the building had been converted into a kitchen and perhaps a buttery. Large numbers of cruck-framed buildings survive in moorland districts, but they are usually hidden from view, behind the stone walls and under the slate roofs that encased them in a later phase of rebuilding.

Late in Queen Elizabeth I's reign, William Camden observed that the western part of Derbyshire was 'barren, but rich in lead yron and coles and also feedeth sheepe very commodiously and plenty of oats'. In 1631 the corn that was harvested in the High Peak was reported to be 'chiefly oats and oatmeal, little other grain growing'. Probate inventories attached to the wills of the inhabitants of Dore and Totley between 1539 and 1644 show that farmers placed far more value on their cattle and sheep than on their cereals. Three out of every four farmers kept small flocks of sheep and most of them had a few dairy cows and stores. Oxen were commonly used as draught animals, but as the seventeenth century progressed farmers turned increasingly to horses. In all, seventy farmers in this sample kept an average seven head of cattle. They were typical of most of the farmers in the moorland townships of the Peak District. In his *The Natural History of Staffordshire* (1686), Robert Plot observed: 'Both Moorelands and Woodlands have goodly Cattle, large and fair spread.'

A glimpse of the common practice of driving cattle and sheep up on to the moors in summertime is provided by a boundary dispute along Stanage and

Moscar in 1724. One witness mentioned 'the Fridley or free ley for the Grass of Hawksworth Common (whereof Moscarr is part)' that was a traditional payment of £4 to the lord of Hallamshire. Another man said that when he was 18 years old, about forty-five or forty-six years previously, he kept 300 sheep for William Greaves of Hathersage parish 'for two Summers between Moscarr Cross and Horderon, and Bradfield parish men saw them and did not disturb them', and George Brownehill recalled that about twenty years previously 'he came to Tent Hatherzidge Cattle upon Moscarr and Tented them for 2 Years and they made him a Cabbin at the end of the Broadrake which he Enjoyed without Interruption while he stay'd'.

Upon the dissolution of the monasteries the Earl of Shrewsbury, lord of Hallamshire and the owner of many Derbyshire properties, bought the Basingwerk Abbey manor of Glossop and Welbeck Abbey's possessions in the Upper Derwent Valley. By 1554 he had sold the former Welbeck Abbey estate to Sir William Cavendish, the new owner of Chatsworth who had been one of King Henry VIII's commissioners when the monasteries were dissolved. In the early seventeenth century this estate was split between Sir William's sons. Hope Woodlands passed to the senior branch at Chatsworth, while the Derwent properties went to the junior branch at Welbeck and Bolsover, who eventually became Dukes of Newcastle. It is our good fortune that both branches of the Cavendish family employed William Senior, one of the most skilled cartographers of his day, to survey these and other estates and to make a superb collection of maps, whose coverage included thousands of acres of moorland landscapes.

In Hope Woodlands, for example, Senior depicted twenty-two dispersed farmsteads in or above the Upper Derwent and Ashop valleys. Most of these stood on or close to the sites of their medieval predecessors. Each of them was surrounded by a small group of irregular-shaped fields, enclosed by drystone walls, with a cattle pasture known as a hey, meaning 'a hedged enclosure', beyond. On the moors above the farmsteads, cattle outpastures and sheepwalks were defined by earthen banks and ditches, most of which can still be traced on the ground. Much of the 16,627 acres of this moorland township consisted of 'bad pasture' or 'out pasture', where the farmers had common rights to dig peat for their fuel. The purpose of some of the holloways that climb up on to the moors is still evident, for they end where they reach the turbaries. Each farmer also had the right to quarry stone for his buildings and field walls, and to gather firewood from the woods in the valleys. The prime importance of grazing on the moorland farms is revealed

These dramatic rocks had acquired their nickname by 1627 when William Senior marked Alperde Castle on his map of this remote Peakland valley. Senior recorded six farms in this part of Hope Woodlands, each with small fields in the valley bottom, cattle heys above and a share of the 1,825-acre outpasture, where sheep were grazed and peat was dug for household fuel.

by some of the other Senior maps. For example, six tenants held 2,450 acres of moorland pasture at Alport, and at Ashop two tenants farmed 5,791 and 350 acres respectively, while another outpasture, covering 1,498 acres and known as the Dean, was shared equally between the farmers at Marebottom, Ridge and Bank Top.

Until the late seventeenth century the medieval chases, or friths, at Rivelin, Loxley and Hawkesworth remained in occasional use for the hunting of deer within Hallamshire. John Harrison's survey of 1637 noted that the 429 acres of Auley Meadows, named after the Hawley family and now known as Hollow Meadows, had been converted to pasture and that the 347 acres of 'A Sheep pasture called Agden lying betweene Agden Common called Cowell' were tenanted at the will of the lord by Richard Broomehead and Edmund Hobson. He also recorded the tenants of the various farms at Howden on the county boundary, where farming was conducted in the same manner as it was across the River Derwent in Derbyshire. The principal tenant was William Greaves, whose farmstead was described as 'a dwelling house of 5 bayes a peate house of 2 bayes a stable of 2 bayes a Barne of 3 bayes another barne 8 bayes & a Kilne of one bay a fold'. Ditches and earthen banks, sometimes surmounted by drystone walls in the lower reaches, enclosed the various fields, cattle heys, sheepwalks, 'outpastures' and turbaries of this 3,245-acre moorland farm. The boundary of the outpasture, which was described in detail, can still be traced along Howden Edge.

It is clear from the Senior and Harrison surveys that large stretches of moorland in Hope Woodlands and the Upper Derwent Valley were private manorial pastures rather than commons. The farmsteads did not share common rights over these moors. Instead, they had well-defined cattle heys and sheepwalks that were regarded as private property. Their rights to graze livestock, dig peat, quarry stone and collect wood were recorded as 'appurtenances' that were attached to the farm rather than as a share of common rights with their neighbours. This explains why these properties on the Yorkshire side of the border did not appear in the Bradfield Enclosure Award nearly two centuries later.

Rights and stints

The phrase 'common rights' did not imply that anyone could graze cattle and sheep on the moors. Such rights were attached to particular farms and were regulated through the manor courts. When the pressure of population grew it became usual for restrictions, or 'stints', to be imposed on the commons according to the number of animals that a farmer could over-winter off the moors. This widespread principle was known to lawyers and writers as 'levancy and couchancy'. A typical 'paine', or penalty, that was agreed at the Holmesfield manor court in 1630 read: 'A payne sett that noe person or persons shall hereafter surcharge the commons by keepinge more beastes and sheep in the summer time than his or their coppihould estates are well able to sustaine, maintaine, and keepe in the winter time.' Anyone who disregarded this order would be fined twenty shillings, a heavy penalty at that time.

The number of livestock that each farmer drove on to the moors at an agreed date in the spring was checked at the lydgate, a swing-gate that provided access from the enclosed land. The Holmesfield moors began at Lydgate Farm, and Lydgate or Lidgett are common minor place-names that are found elsewhere on the moorland edges. In 1706 an agreement was made to stint the grazing of sheep, horses and cattle on the commons of Chapel-en-le-Frith: 'Suppose 5 Sheep to a whole Beast, A Beast and halfe to a Horse so in proportion to all Younger Cattel & horses. And 2 Sheep gates to every Pound according to their accustomed Rents or value of their respective Lands, Farms &c.'

A case brought before the Court of Chancery in 1676 illustrates the pressures on the moorland commons within the Graveship of Holme and elsewhere. Humphrey Bray, a Hepworth yeoman copyholder, was said to have entered into an agreement with his neighbour, Oliver Roberts of Ox Lee, about 'a certain Common for the depastureing of sheep and other Catle for the Farmers owners or occupiers of their respective Farmes' about eighteen years previously, but he had not abided by it since. Bray's defence was that he and Roberts 'hapned to be drinking in an Alehouse together and after they had drunke much drinke they fell into discourse about a certain Common for the depastureing of sheep and other cattle and how the same was overstocked with sheep', and that 'being hot with drinking and scarce understanding what he said or did' he may have made some promise to Roberts and have signed a £50 bond, but he was illiterate.

The ruins of Ox Lee Farm mark the 'ox-clearing' at the limits of cultivation in the medieval Graveship of Holme. The local surname Oxley is derived from this farm. The 1676 dispute over the amount of livestock on the Hepworth commons concerned this property.

Roberts had died three years previously but he had never stopped Bray from pasturing his animals, nor had he mentioned the bond, but his widow had married Jonas Kay, a Holmfirth yeoman, who was now pressing the case. Bray claimed that he did not mean to extinguish his rights, but merely to agree to 'some certain stint as to the number of sheep to be depastured' on the common 'called the law, the harden and the mosse betweixt the law and the harden'. We do not know the outcome of the case, but Bray asserted that without this common right of grazing it would be impossible for him and other farmers there 'to manure and manage their respective Farmes and lands'.

In 1650 a survey of Eckington manor, which at that time still had large moors or commons, recorded the common rights of the freeholders and tenants on about 1,000 acres as: 'Common of Herbage or Pasture for Summer Feeding within Tenn Oxgang of Land. Copyholders have Common of Herbage for all manner of Cattle; dig or Cutt Clodds and Earth and to cutt down Whinnes Hollice and Gorse; digg and sell Coales; Cutt down and fell for their own use, or to make Sale of all Woods and Underwoods growing upon their Coppyhold Lands; have Tymber and Stone within the Lord's Wastgrounds (as often as need shall require) for the repairing of their House; Common of Herbage at all tymes of the Yeare for all Manor of Cattle within two Springe Woods [Lightwood and Common Wood]. Commons and Waste Grounds: Eckington Marsh, Bramley Moore, Ridgeway Moore, Plumbley Wood, Base Green, Eckington Leyes, Mosborough Moore, Little Moore, Spinckhill Moore and Emmett Carrs.'

Further north, the manor of Worsbrough contained 100 acres of gorse and heath and 300 acres of moorland, with the right to pasture animals and to collect wood, gorse and bracken for building or for fuel. It was in everybody's interest that vermin and predators should be destroyed. The churchwardens' accounts for Worsbrough parish for 1708–30 include payments for the killing of foxes, fourmarts (polecats), otters, urchins (hedgehogs), weevils, badgers, moles and sparrows. Contemporary accounts for Ecclesfield parish note the destruction of foxes, badgers (known as bawsons or grays), fourmarts, urchins, a wild cat, bullfinches and crows, and in Derbyshire the Hope churchwardens' accounts for 1686–7 record payments for the heads of ten foxes, five fox cubs, fourteen badgers, twenty-five ravens and 205 hedgehogs, and in 1739–40 for three otters.

Another common right allowed the gathering of bracken and moss from the moors, particularly for use as winter bedding for horses and cattle. This practice is mentioned in a dispute over the boundaries on the moors above the River Derwent in 1724, when Joseph Halgreave, aged 63, said that '50 years agoe his Father Bought of Mr Green Mr Peggs agent the Liberty of Burning Brackin upon Moscarr anywhere between Moscarr Cross and Bamford Moore which he did for 3 years without Interruption'. The harvesting of bracken was regulated carefully and restrictions were placed on its burning to produce potash. In 1780, for instance, the Holmesfield manor court resolved to 'lay a pain on any person, or persons, that shall hereafter, burn bracken before Old St James's Day [25 July]; for any such default to forfeit the sum of ten shillings to the lord of the manor'.

Rushbearing was a flourishing custom in the High Peak, for example at Chapel-en-le-Frith and Glossop, where carts loaded with rushes and decked with flowers and ribbons were brought down from the moors to strew over the floors of the churches and chapels. In the Graveship of Holme, Arthur Jessop noted in his diary the rushbearing at the dissenting chapel at Lydgate on 25 July 1743 and another such event at the Anglican chapel at Holmfirth

This Anglican chapel-of-ease near Toot Hill in a remote part of Macclesfield Forest was founded in 1673 but was entirely rebuilt in 1834. Each August the ancient tradition of rushbearing is still observed.

on 6 September 1744: 'There was a Rushbearing from Hades to Holmfirth and Mr Harrop kept them out and they had a great stir to get into the Chapel.' The Revd John Harrop was a young man who had been chosen as the minister at Holmfirth the previous year and who frowned on this ancient rural practice. At Slaithwaite, too, the Revd Robert Meeke wrote in his diary for 30 August 1691 that his congregation was small as many young people went to Meltham, Marsden and Ripponden, 'being the first Sunday after their Rushbearings'. When the same thing happened the following year, he commented: 'Such is the vanity of the times.' The custom is still observed each August at St Stephen's, the Forest Chapel high above Macclesfield.

Peat

The heather moorlands have been much reduced in size over the centuries by the cutting of peat for domestic and industrial fuel. Paul Ardron has shown that virtually all the blanket peats on the edges of the moors have been affected by cutting. Large areas now covered by grasslands, mostly of the *Molinia* and *Nardus* varieties, were given their present appearance by families that exercised their common right of turbary in the summer months in order to have sufficient fuel for winter.

The traveller from Holmesfield to Owler Bar is greeted with the sight of a group of holloways rising up the moor behind the Peacock Inn. A climb up one of these holloways soon demonstrates their particular purpose. It becomes clear that they are not part of a thoroughfare across the moors, for once the summit is reached, near the old shepherd's meeting cairn that has been converted in recent years into a landmark, they peter out. The heather disappears and all that lies ahead is flat grassland, where the peat has been dug away. Only the name Totley Moss hints at its former character.

This is a common experience on the Peak District moors. At Edale, the first part of the Pennine Way that follows the old peat track up on to the moor at Grindslow Knoll before turning towards Kinder Scout vanishes once the former turbary is reached. This track is remembered in the village as the route whereby peat was brought down on sledges to burn in the fire grates of the farmsteads and cottages. The creation of many another moorland holloway can be explained in this way. For example, a 'Turfegaite' was recorded within the Graveship of Holme in 1540.

The usual custom at the turbaries was to remove the top sods and pile them on one side, so that when the peat was removed they could be replaced and the land restored for grazing. In 1570 a by-law issued by the Slaithwaite manor court, just beyond the Peak District, ordered each tenant to 'dig the lowest Turffe and clear out his own pits and take up the Topp Soddes or heap them properly'. The old turbaries can sometimes be recognised by their vertical edges around the regular depressions that were cut into the peat. In some places, such as near Derwent Edge, it is possible to discern the dry baulks that once divided the turbaries into sections, so that the rights associated with each farm would not be disputed. A 6-feet high boundary balk on Peat Moor, on the slopes of Edale Valley, seems to have divided the Upper Booth and Barber Booth turbaries. Other surviving features that are difficult, if not impossible, to date include loading bays and drains such as those that were specified in the Holmesfield manor court on 23 April 1624: 'A paine Sett that no person or persons shall dig, or make any Peate Pitts upon the moore, but, immediately after the getting of such peate, slytt the same whereby the water may issue forth.'

Tenants of a manor were also penalised if their drains and watercourses overflowed into the turf gates. In 1584 John Hadfield of Holme was fined in the local manor court because he 'diverted a water course into the common road for bringing in the turf'. And in neighbouring Hepworth in 1640 it was ordered that nobody had the right to 'digg or grave turves or sods within four yards of the hyway'. In Holme in 1639 every householder was expected to go 'to the mending of the turfe gaites ... upon indifferent warnings' or else to 'send a sufficient labourer'. Turf was used not just for fuel but as a roofing material and for bedding animals. In 1664 the Graveship of Holme section of the Wakefield manor court recorded a carriage way from Cartworth Moor that was used between 1 November and 1 March for leading 'beddinge turfes'.

Networks of sledways connected the turbaries to individual farms or hamlets. A prominent group of holloways descend from the Upper Derwent moors to Grainfoot Farm, Tinker's House and Derwent hamlet, where the peat was stored in barns or special turf houses. The sparse documentary evidence that survives includes that contained in the probate inventories attached to the wills of some of the farmers. For example, Edward Barber of Ronksley (1679) had '2 peat sleds, 2 pair of peat sides, a sled rope and 3 pairs of sled legs'; Ralph Sanderson of Upper Midhope, yeoman (1697), owned equipment valued at £1 in his turf house; and Thomas Barlow of Holdsworth, husbandman (1719), possessed 'a Turfe Cart'.

Many a moorland turbary was difficult to reach. At Crookstone Moor, on the eastern side of Kinder Scout, one of the deepest and most expansive turbaries in the Peak District covered about 500 acres. This was the principal source of fuel for the inhabitants of the township of Hope some 5 miles distant over very uneven tracks. On this moor, parts of the face of the peat were about 6 feet high. 'Turves' or 'Peats' were cut, with a little inclining, into rectangles, 12 inches long, 6 inches broad and 2 inches thick. When first cut, the turves were very soft and wet, and so were left in stacks to dry and harden, then set on end against each other to dry more thoroughly before they were brought home on sledges.

In the Graveship of Holme, where peat was plentiful on the northern edge of the Peak District, the manorial grave reported tenants from other districts who were caught digging turves there. In the fifteenth century these were often men from Shepley, further east, who had little peat of their own, but it seems that their modest fines were simply a roundabout way of paying for this privilege. In nearby Meltham, which also possessed large stretches of moorland, tenants from outside the lordship were allowed to dig turf for 'their fire in their house' but were fined 3s.4d. a cart-load for anything in excess of this. Turbary rights on smaller moors were much more strenuously contested.

When John Farey published the third volume of his report on the agriculture of Derbyshire in 1817, he observed that peat was 'a great deal

This group of holloways on Crookstone Moor, climbing the eastern slopes of Kinder Scout, were used by the inhabitants of Hope to exercise their common right of turbary at a considerable distance from their village.

less used now as fuel than formerly', because coal could be transported long distances on the turnpike roads. Nevertheless, when the Graveship of Holme was enclosed in 1834 the commissioners set aside 40 acres so that poor tenants could continue to enjoy their right of turbary, and an account from Abney in 1888–89 noted that William Redfearn was paid £1.3s.0d. for 'Gravel, Peat & Turf Getting'. Peat remained a major source of fuel in the remoter districts well into Victorian times.

Early enclosure of the commons

The decline of the great medieval lordships and ecclesiastical estates, culminating in the dissolution of the monasteries, brought other changes to the farming systems of the moorland edges. At Horton Hay, north-west of Leek, for example, a tract of woodland pasture was converted into eight dairy farms. Elsewhere in that district, the former vaccaries became indistinguishable from neighbouring farms, and the communal strips of the townfields were enclosed by numerous private agreements and converted into permanent or temporary pastures. Often this was a long, drawn-out process.

The purchasers of former monastic granges were keen to raise rents and exert what they saw as their rights, even if the memory of these was preserved only in the old documents that their lawyers had read meticulously. Long before the dissolution of the monasteries, peasant farmers had vigorously disputed the right of a lessee of a grange to pasture large flocks of sheep on the common wastes. Now, they resorted to litigation or to rioting when a new owner tried to enclose a sheepwalk. They also resisted the lessees of the Duchy of Lancaster estates and the lords of other manors within the High Peak who attempted to raise the level of entry fines and rents to match or exceed inflation. Even the mightiest lords did not always get their own way. In a celebrated case of 1579 the tenants of the manors of Ashford, the Forest of the Peak and Glossop Dale were victorious when they went to London to contest the actions of George, sixth Earl of Shrewsbury, who was mortified when the Privy Council ruled in their favour.

When new lords attempted to enclose parts of the Staffordshire Moorlands they met with fierce resistance. In 1568 about 100 men from Longnor forcibly asserted their rights on Fawfield Hill by demolishing fences that had been erected there. A subsequent award stipulated that the part of the hill nearest Longnor was to remain open to them and to the tenants of four farms in Heathylee whose land bordered it. The Longnor men were also given an eighty-year lease of a quarter of the enclosed part of the hill, for which each householder was to pay the lord 4d. and a hen every year.

When the Lords of Bradnop made several attempts to enclose parts of Morridge in the sixteenth, seventeenth and early eighteenth centuries, the freeholders of Bradnop objected to such large-scale projects, though they agreed the waste needed to be protected from outsiders. About 240 acres were enclosed in the 1650s, but the Staffordshire JPs insisted that every cottager should be given four acres so that they would not become a burden on the poor rates. This dispute between lord and tenants dragged on into the next century. Much of Morridge remained open until the remaining 3,139 acres of the Bradnop and Onecote commons and wastes were enclosed by Act of Parliament in 1766–69.

Enclosure did not always provoke heated arguments, however. Much was agreed upon peacefully by lords and tenants. New farms advanced steadily up the escarpments during the sixteenth, seventeenth and eighteenth centuries under the control of the manor courts. Whereas in 1709 the various commons and wastes within the Graveship of Holme were estimated at 14,280 acres, by 1834, on the eve of parliamentary enclosure, they had been reduced to 9,200 acres. In this way, the rising population was accommodated and fed, but much of the difficult, unproductive land that was enclosed from the moorland wastes during this time has long since been abandoned.

Alstonefield parish contained a large area of moorland waste which provided rough grazing. Cottagers were allowed to settle there and to improve the waste by their own efforts and expense. The policy of increasing rents as the cottagers' income grew encouraged the settlement of a district 'which holds out as few natural temptations perhaps as any part of England'. By the end of the eighteenth century many cottagers who had extended their holdings paid only small rents or nothing at all and Sir Henry Harpur, the descendant of the Harpurs of Swarkestone and later of Calke Abbey who had acquired most of the manor in the seventeenth century, was advised by his lawyers not to disturb them. A steady process of both legal and illegal encroachment on the edges of the moors is also evident from a parliamentary survey of 1650, which noted that the section of the Forest of the Peak that was known as Bowden Middlecale contained sixty-nine 'certain small cottages and little parcels of ground called intacks encroached upon the waste ground', and that twenty-two of these were illegal encroachments.

This aerial view of the hamlet of Rough Birchworth in the parish of Penistone shows how the open fields were enclosed by the agreement of the farmers in the seventeenth or eighteenth centuries simply by building walls along some of the old strip boundaries. Their long, narrow pattern makes a sharp contrast with the rectangular fields that were created when the commons and wastes beyond were enclosed in 1818–26. (Photograph: Courtesy of Meridian Airmaps Ltd.)

The commons and wastes of the Forest of the Peak were graded into the best, middle and worst sorts, with the best used for summer grazing by cattle and the remainder left to the sheep. Royal attempts to dismantle the Forest of the Peak, in order to reduce the Crown's financial problems, began in the 1630s but were not completed until the late seventeenth century. In 1673 the commons and wastes of the manors of High Peak and Castleton were divided between the Duchy of Lancaster and the freeholders, despite the opposition of the poorer inhabitants. The Duchy's officers leased their share to tenant farmers, who immediately introduced large flocks of sheep. This was followed by the enclosure of the commons and wastes of Hope and other parts of the High Peak in 1675, and those of Castleton in 1691. A unanimous resolution to enclose 153 acres of pasturage at Eyam in 1702 made the freeholders 'very well pleased contented and satisfied'.

Upon this enclosure of thousands of acres of commons and wastes in the High Peak, the landscape was transformed by new farms, walls, cart tracks and lanes, many of which survive to this day. An enclosure agreement that was made in 1640 between the Duchy of Lancaster and over eighty freeholders in Bowden Middlecale, in the Chapel-en-le-Frith and New Mills district, was thwarted by the Civil War, but maps made at the time show that the present walls coincide exactly with the boundaries of the various hamlets and with the divisions between the parts that were allotted equally to the Crown and the freeholders. The enclosure scheme was revived in 1674 and the Crown's half-share was granted on a long-term lease to Thomas Eyre of Rowtor Hall, near Winster. One of his new creations was the 127-acre Piece Farm on Ollersett Moor, 800 feet above sea level. The freeholders and tenants obtained a final decree concerning their half-share in 1711, but they delayed enclosing it into separate parcels until they obtained private Acts of Parliament in the nineteenth century.

Greens and small commons

In the western townships of Hallamshire the scattered farmsteads and hamlets, ascending towards open moorland, were often arranged around or at the side of a green or a small common. Documentary evidence for these greens is hard to come by. In the ancient parish of Sheffield they were not recorded until the second half of the sixteenth century, although by that time some of them may have been ancient. Perhaps they were documented only after farmhouses or cottages had been erected alongside them. Some of these buildings may have been constructed on medieval assarts, others on intakes that were cleared upon the recovery of the national population in Elizabethan or Jacobean times. By the eighteenth century, all these greens and small commons had settlements strung around or alongside them. John Gelley's map of Ecclesall in 1725, for example, marks buildings clustered alongside Little Common, Oakes Green and Bents Green on the north-western side of Ecclesall Woods.

Manorial records occasionally suggest approximate dates for some of these encroachments, for they record entry fines and annual rents, at least for the legal ones. In 1578, for example, the Court Leet of the Manor of Sheffield noted that at Owlerton 'Robert Shawe hath builded a lytle house of the Lordes waste there conteyninge one Bay for the which he doth paye yearly the Rent of iiijd.'

After the passing of the Act of Settlement in 1665, however, the erection of cottages on the wastes became a matter of concern for the parish or township overseers of the poor as well as the officers of the manor. In 1685, for instance, Christopher Lee, labourer, and Robert Glossop, mason, were charged at the Ecclesall manor court with 'erecting a Cottage upon the Common in the night without lawful leave', and in 1718 Thomas Colley was fined 'for erecting a Cottage at Crookesmoorside'. Shrinking commons reduced the grazing and diminished the other rights of the commoners. In 1718 the Ecclesall manor court insisted on the custom of levancy and couchancy by agreeing that none 'shall keep more Sheep upon the Commons in Summer time than they can keep on their Inlands in winter'. Seven years later, when a visitor saw a cutler's grinding wheel that had been erected on common land by the River Sheaf, he was told that 'this common or moor has been of late years much enclosed'.

Woods

During the seventeenth century the fashion for hunting declined so much that the deer were eventually removed from the forests and chases. When Gilbert, the seventh Earl of Shrewsbury, died in 1616 the Lords of Hallamshire ceased to reside at Sheffield Manor Lodge and rarely visited their lordship. In the late seventeenth century the remaining deer in the moorland chases of Rivelin, Loxley and Hawksworth were slaughtered and most of the great woods were felled. In 1637 John Harrison had observed that visitors had 'not seen such Timber in Cristendome' as that which adorned Hall Park on the Stannington side of the Rivelin Valley, but in 1662, when John Evelyn published his great work *Sylva*, the valley was said to be 'totally destitute' of its former glorious oaks. In the mid-eighteenth century John Wilson, the antiquary of Broomhead Hall, noted in his journal that 'Riveling was formerly full of wood and a chace of Red Deer therein'.

The removal of the deer and the use of new fodder crops for sheep meant that holly was no longer needed as a winter feed. As late as 1697, Abraham de la Pryme noted in his diary: 'In the South West of Yorkshire, at and about Bradfield and in Darbishire, they feed all their sheep in winter with holly leaves and bark … To every farm there are so many holly trees, and the more there is the farm is dearer, but care is taken to plant great number thereabouts.' The evidence for the cultivation of 'haggs' of 'hollins' on the moorland edges goes back well into the Middle Ages, but peters out in the 1720s. In 1710 the Duke of Norfolk's bailiff had reported that several holly haggs were unlet and mostly destroyed, but two years later the duke's woodward paid a man four shillings for going on horseback for two days 'in the Great Snow to see if anyone Cropped Holling'. The last record of the use of holly in the manor court rolls occurs in 1737, when a Bradfield man agreed to lease 'all the hag of Hollin called Ugghill Wood'. Only a few minor place-names now commemorate this former widespread practice. Later in the eighteenth century, hollies were used for making bird lime. In 1777, for example, 'the bark of 937 holly trees in Bolsterstone' was sold for £150, and around the same time the Duke of Devonshire's Hope Woodlands estate reserved the right, when offering farm leases, to 'carry away what turves and peats he or they shall want for boiling holly bark'.

In the 1770s the tenants of the Hope Woodlands farms were allowed to 'stub and effectively grub and cut up by the roots all the wood which shall from time to time grow or sprout from old roots in or upon the said farms, save and except as such parts thereof as have already been coppiced or shall hereafter be coppiced'. It was normal practice to preserve the coppice woods from the effects of grazing while the trees were young but to open them to livestock once they were mature. Their principal use was for making charcoal. Numerous charcoal platforms have been identified in the Upper Derwent Valley and on the sides of the cloughs that descend into it, particularly in Grimbocar Wood, Rough Wood, Fearfall Wood, Lee Wood, Hagg Side and Nabs Wood, and on the eastern side of the valley in the chapelry of Bradfield. These platforms are characteristically 4–8 metres long and 2.5 metres wide and they can be recognised from the blackened earth and small pieces of hard charcoal. In the middle decades of the eighteenth century the Duke of Devonshire sold rights to make charcoal in Hope Woodlands to the South Yorkshire ironmasters of Attercliffe Forge, Wortley Top Forge and Mousehole Forge.

In 1771 John Wilson, the antiquary, jotted down the reminiscences of old John Horsfield, who remembered the final removal of the deer from the Ewden Valley and the felling of several hundred yew trees, which were sold to Sheffield cutlers to make into knife hafts. Only the curled parts of the yews were used in this way; the rest was felled and burnt by the tenants in order to create new pastures. An undated manuscript in the British Library noted that the 'great quantities of Red Deer' which had formerly grazed in the valley were: 'accustomed to do great damage to the corn growing at Broomhead, Wightwisle, and other places thereabouts; so much so that they were forced to hire tenters to make lodges for looking after the same which names divers doles and roods in the Byerdole townfield now retain as Tenter Dole, Lodge Dole, etc.' Successive generations of the Greaves family served as deer keeper at Ewden Lodge.

Industries

In the sixteenth, seventeenth and eighteenth centuries the parish of Hathersage was the main centre of millstone hewing in the Peak District. The quarries on Stanage, Millstone Edge, Reeve's Edge, Yarncliff and some smaller delves were all exploited, and several other gritstone edges, such as Baslow Edge, Gardom's Edge and the escarpment above Chatsworth Park, retain evidence on the ground of former use. However, the industry remained relatively small-scale and even the large quarries were not worked

Bole Hill millstones, near Surprise View. No purchaser could be found when these millstones were hewn in the 1920s or 1930s and so they stay by the loading bay amongst the bracken. They are in various shapes and sizes and were designed for pulping wood into paper or grinding paint rather than for corn milling.

continuously. John Wilson, the antiquary of Broomhead Hall, noted, for instance, that about the year 1710 work at the Rivelin Valley quarries was discontinued: 'since when the Mill Stone Edge near Hathersedge, has been in vogue. Mr. Rotherham has taken this in Riveling and will not let it be worked lest it should damage the sale of the other.' This was John Rotherham of Dronfield Hall, whose family rose to gentry status through their enterprise in smelting lead and exporting millstones over three generations.

A tithe dispute in 1590 reveals that thirteen hewers were then at work in Hathersage parish, each of them making twelve pairs a year, or one a fortnight. This combined effort amounted to the manufacture of over 300 millstones a year. The hewers were paid about 10d. a week, which was comparable to the wages earned by other craftsmen at the time, but many of them were part-time farmers, so the millstone work was not continuous. The hey-day of the Peak District trade, when local millstones were exported to many different parts of the land, was from the second half of the seventeenth century until the Victorian era when water mills and windmills were gradually replaced by roller milling at the ports and composite stones were preferred to those made from millstone grit.

In 1673 Richard Blome wrote that Derbyshire had 'great quarries, out of which Mill-stones are got, also Grindstones, and Scyth-stones, which imploy many hands in working up, and are dispersed over great part of the Nation'. And in 1692 John Houghton observed that Derbyshire had 'rich Quarries of Mill-stones and they served most parts of the Kingdom, and they are worth 8, 9 or 10 pounds the Pair, and Grindstones of all sorts, from 5 or 6 Foot Diameter and under, and Scythe-stones in abundance, which serve all parts of the Kingdom'. Blome also noted that Bawtry, the nearest inland port for Peak District products, had 'a great trade for Mill-stones and Grindstones', which were taken down the Rivers Idle and Trent.

Most of the abandoned millstones that can be found in profusion in the quarries and loading bays of Hathersage parish were made in the late nineteenth and early twentieth centuries for industrial purposes, such as pulping wood into paper or grinding paint, but some older stones that were designed for corn milling can be recognised by their convex shape. They were left where they were made when a serious flaw was discovered. A few have the owner's mark, usually in the form of an initial, inscribed upon them.

Hewers knew from experience how to choose a suitably shaped rock. Erasmus Darwin explained in 1795 how they proceeded: 'It is usual in separating large millstones from the silicious sand rocks in some parts of Derbyshire, to bore horizontal holes under them in a circle, and fill these with pegs made from dry wood which gradually swell by the moisture of the earth, and, in a day or two, lift up the millstone without breaking it.' On average it took ten days to finish a millstone. 'Peak' or 'Grey' millstones were used for grinding the inferior grains: oats, barley, peas and beans. They could not compete with German or French stones when it came to fine grinding but were commonly used for the rougher work that sufficed for other grains. They were dressed, or 'feathered', by the miller, not in the quarry. A pair of Derbyshire stones could grind about 100 tons of grain, so if a flour mill was constantly at work, the stones had to be dressed once every three weeks or so. But most country mills managed with dressing their stones only twice a year.

The holloways that descend from the quarries on a regular incline to the highways were dug out by men employed by the quarry owners. They can rarely be dated precisely, but one that descends from Offerton Moor towards Hathersage was constructed in the summer of 1722, 'so as the milne stones might pass'. They are remembered as horse-drawn sledge roads, but in some cases carts or wagons may have been used. In the mid-eighteenth century, John Wilson noted in his journal:

> The road to the new blew slate delph at Cartledge was begun by Mr. George Smilter of Sheffield on Monday, 28th May 1750 & cut thro: the moss in many places three yards deep in twelve weeks time, seldom having under twelve & never more than twenty six men employed. The cut is about a mile & half long the deepest place about a yard and a half deep, the deepest places about 100 yards long each. The first waggon that came for slate was Richard Wilson's of Castle Fould, Sheffield. A good deal of the slate was sent to London & other places, was very fine and light but would not stand the weather. There has been none got many years'. A lease from the Duke of Norfolk, dated 27 March 1750, gave this George Smilter of Sheffield, wheelwright, the right to get slate-stones and 'paviors' in and around 'a place called Howden Chest or Cartledge with liberty to take and carry away the same through all convenient ways and passages to be made upon the Moors.

The route traverses one of the loneliest parts of the Dark Peak, from high above Abbey Clough along the Duke of Norfolk's road to Bar Dyke in the chapelry of Bradfield. It is now badly worn and weathered, but it can still be followed on the ground.

The parish of Saddleworth was famous for the quality of its bakestones, flat stones that could be placed on or next to a fire to cook oatcakes. The trade was a medieval one, for the poll tax returns of 1379 for Quick quarter name a John Bakestonman. Two quarries – the old and the new – that were sold to the Gartside family in 1543 lay beside the Hull Brook within the Friarmere quarter of the parish. The small settlement of Delph took its name from the lower one. On 8 October 1733 John Hobson of Dodworth Green, near Barnsley, went: 'to Delph in Friarmere, in the parish of Saddleworth … It is there that all the havercake backstones are got out of a quarry, the only one I have heard of in England. The mine lies on the side of a hill, and is about eight yards thick, and about three yards of earth to clear on it.'

Bar Brook smelting mill. Lead that was mined in the White Peak was brought across the Eastern Moors to be smelted by water power in the valleys created by streams and rivers. David Crossley and David Kiernan have shown that the first lead mill on this site was built in 1618 by Robert Mower of Millthorpe and that in 1679 it was operated by John Broomhead of Bubnell, who obtained his ore from Taddington, Monyash, Over Haddon and Hassop, and who exported finished pigs of lead via the river port at Bawtry. The lead mill closed around 1770, when it was replaced with a cupola and slag-mill further down the brook. In Victorian times the site was used for a flour mill. The pond survives and ore slag can be found between the earthworks of the mill and the stream.

The Peak District's major industry at this time was the mining and smelting of lead. By Elizabethan times, the Derbyshire lead field was the most prosperous in Europe. The lead ore that was mined in the White Peak during the hey-day of the industry was smelted in the river valleys further east. By the 1580s, the old bole hills on the windy moorland escarpments had been replaced by a new method of smelting that used water-powered bellows to heat white coal, produced from coppiced woods, to a high temperature. The major smelting sites were in the wooded valleys between Sheffield and Chesterfield, but others can be found on the edges of the moors, where brooks and streams could be converted into ponds. For example, a remote site at North Lees below Stanage Edge was used to smelt lead from the last quarter of the seventeenth century until the 1760s, when it was converted to the making of paper.

Another moorland site, on the Bar Brook before its steep descent into Baslow, was marked as a smelting mill on Burdett's map of Derbyshire in 1767. Soon afterwards these smelting mills were replaced by coal-fired reverberatory furnaces known as cupolas, which could use lower grades of ore on any suitable site, including moorland ones such as Ringinglow to the west of Sheffield.

Coal mining too was a minor activity for the inhabitants of the moorlands. Small drift mines that descended to shallow seams were in use along both the western and eastern edges of the gritstones; from the Staffordshire Moorlands to Buxton and beyond, and from Hallamshire to Holmfirth. In 1709, for instance, the Wakefield Manor Book noted 'A Coliery on Lawmoor in Holmfirth farmed by Jonas Kay, Gent' at a £2 yearly rent. In some cases, these seams were mined until as late as the 1950s or 1960s.

In northern parts of the Peak District the main extra source of income came from the textile industry. For example, in 1694 John Radcliffe of New Mills, yeomen, had two pairs of looms and a dyeing lead. Several yeomen farmsteads in the north-west were rebuilt in stone in the late seventeenth or early eighteenth centuries, notably the one that John Hyde erected at Long Lee, Rowarth, in 1663. Later in the century Edward Bower, a yeoman-clothier and woollen draper of Torr Top in Whittle, built a new house. The finishing and sale of woollen cloth long remained the family's main source of income, but the business was expanded by his second son Thomas, who owned a fulling mill, paper mill and tannery.

On the other side of the Pennines the making of woollen cloth was a useful by-employment in the chapelry of Bradfield and the parish of Penistone. Coarse, narrow cloths known as 'Ordinary Penistones' were made as far back as 1468–9 and were frequently referred to in the Elizabethan period, when they were sold by Wakefield merchants at Blackwell Hall, London. As late as the 1720s, Daniel Defoe included 'Penistones' in his description of the famous Stourbridge Fair, near Cambridge. In 1743 a cloth fair was first held in the upper rooms of the grammar school at Penistone, and twenty years later a cloth hall, paid for by public subscription, was erected in the market square and the owners of the three local fulling mills agreed to refuse any cloth that was not sold there. The agreement was signed by ninety-two clothiers.

Penistone parish lay on the southern edge of the West Riding textile district, but further north, in the Graveship of Holme, Meltham and Marsden, the dual occupation of the farmer-clothier was the normal way of life. The 100 or so probate inventories that have survived for the Graveship of Holme between 1690 and 1762 show how most households combined the running of a small farm with the production of cloth. All the men described as clothiers had farm stock and nearly all the husbandmen and yeomen were involved in the cloth trade. Only the poorest weavers had no smallholding.

Apart from the fulling process, the weekly manufacture of a piece of cloth was completed by the combined efforts of the family. The children prepared the wool by beating and carding it, spinning was a woman's job, and the men did the weaving in upstairs chambers, which had long ranges of windows to allow the maximum amount of light to fall on the looms. The typical product of the narrow loom was the cheap woollen kersey, which was not normally dyed. Northern dozens were made on the broad looms, but they were replaced in the eighteenth century by 'Leeds Reds', a coarse cloth that was slightly finished and sent to the dressing shops of the Leeds merchants. The completed piece was scoured with stale urine, which was stored as 'wash' in large pots, then the piece was rinsed thoroughly before it was taken to be thickened at the fulling mill, then taken home to be dried and stretched on tenter frames in the back gardens.

Most of these farmer-clothiers on the edge of the moors shared the same standard of living. A hearth tax return of 1664 shows that 111 of the 437 householders in the Graveship of Holme were exempt from payment and that 269 of the tax payers had only one hearth and forty-two had just two. Richard Allott, the corn miller, paid the most tax, on five hearths.

Communications

In 1698 Celia Fiennes, journeying on horseback through the Peak District, commented on 'the steepness and hazard of the Wayes – if you take a wrong Way there is no passing – you are forced to have Guides as in all parts of Derbyshire'. A generation earlier, when Edward and Thomas Browne crossed the moors between Chesterfield and Chatsworth on a stormy day in September 1662, they were thankful to have Bakewell men to guide them over 'this strange mountainous, misty, moorish, rocky, wild country'. They were astonished at 'the great quantity of rain that fell [which] came down in floods from the tops of the hills, washing downe mud and so making a bog in every valley, the craggy ascents, the rocky unevenness of the roade, the high peaks and the almost perpendicular descents, that we were to ride down'. This is how visitors from the south of England viewed the moors, but local men too had their fears. When the Nonconformist parson and apothecary, Revd James Clegg of Chapel-en-le-Frith, arrived at Baslow on 5 February 1735, he wrote in his diary that 'a kind providence directed me safely over the East more and I got in in good time'.

Nevertheless, the moors to the east of the River Derwent are criss-crossed with old tracks that provide much physical evidence of their regular use, in the form of holloways, causeys, bridges and waymarkers. The moorland

The building of this bridge in the hamlet of Derwent was authorised by the Derbyshire JPs in 1683, but it was removed in 1942 upon the construction of the Ladybower reservoir and in 1959 was re-sited at Slippery Stones, 4 miles upstream.

This paved way that climbs up the Stanage escarpment from North Lees in the parish of Hathersage is a typical causey of the packhorse era. The term is derived from the Norman French *caucie* and is still used in local speech.

holloways tend to be less deep than those that were confined to a particular line through a wood or along the boundary of a field, for the choice of route was unrestricted. Often, a series of tracks, now partly buried under the heather, fan out over a wide area. Numerous shallow holloways can be traced on the Big Moor, but similar features are scarce on Kinder, Bleaklow and the northern mosses, which were difficult to cross even in summer time. Deep holloways – other than those that were cut out to move millstones – are comparatively rare on the moors, except where they descend the steepest hills. They are far more common in the neighbouring cultivated districts, such as the Cordwell Valley in the townships of Holmesfield and Barlow. The same is true of the lines of flagstones known as causeys, which on the moors were mostly confined to busy routes or to particular difficult terrain.

    An unusual record of a Pennine crossing is provided by Arthur Jessop of Lydgate, near Holmfirth, when Bonnie Prince Charlie's Highlanders invaded England. On 29 November 1745 he wrote in his diary: 'It is reported this day that the Rebels are for leaving Lancashire and are for coming into Yorkshire and so come by Woodhead, and they are for pulling up Holm Causeway to hinder any of them from coming over Holm moss, and some say they have pulled it up.' Nineteen months later the inhabitants of Holmfirth were presented at the quarter sessions for allowing 2,000 yards of their causey at Holme Moss to fall into 'great ruin and decay'.

When the amount of wheeled traffic increased during the seventeenth and eighteenth centuries, the medieval bridges, such as those that span the River Derwent at Cromford, Matlock and Darley, were widened to twice their original size by order of the Justices of the Peace meeting at quarter sessions. This was also the time when the wooden bridges across small rivers and streams were replaced by the sturdy, stone-built packhorse bridges that still adorn the landscape on and just off the moors. Some of these were erected by private individuals, but most were paid for out of the local rates. On the moors, simple slab bridges, resting on firm foundations, sometimes sufficed, as on two crossings of the Bar Brook on the Big Moor.

An Act of Parliament of 1697 authorised JPs to order the construction of guide stoops in remote places where the increasing numbers of travellers had difficulty in finding their way. The finest collections of these stoops are found in the Peak District, the western parts of the West Riding, and on the North York Moors. The Derbyshire JPs took the lead in 1709 by ordering the erection of 'a Stone or Post with an inscription theron in large Letters, containing the Name of the next Market Town to which each of the said joyning Highways leads'.

Many of the Derbyshire stoops have the date 1709 and a pointing hand inscribed on them. Several others were erected after a new order in 1737. The earliest West Riding stoops, of 1733–34, were sometimes inscribed with the names of villages and hamlets as well as the nearest market towns, then in 1738 the JPs ordered that new stoops should have miles recorded on them. These measurements were customary miles of about 2,200 yards, or a mile-and-a-quarter in modern reckoning, rather than the statutory mile of 1,760 yards.

A variety of guide stoops, dating from 1709, mark old routes across the Peak District moors. On Brampton Moor pointing hands indicate the ways to Chesterfield and Sheffield.

The Peak District's surviving guide stoops, bridges, causeys and holloways provide invaluable evidence of the routes that crossed the moors in the era before turnpike roads and parliamentary enclosure. They show that the moors were not the impenetrable barrier to communication that is often supposed.

Nor is it true, as is sometimes asserted, that carts were unknown in the Peak District at this time. In 1688 Thomas Peake of Peak Forest owned a corn cart, and in 1712 Francis Vernon of Sparrowpit Gate, a husbandman and clothier, had 'Two Carts and one pair of Wheels' as well as 'Three Mares and their Carrying Gears'. The smaller wain had long been a familiar vehicle in moorland districts.

The growing economy

The growth of trade in the late seventeenth and early eighteenth centuries resulted in improved communications and the establishment of weekly markets and annual fairs in many of the settlements around the edges of the moors. In 1714, for instance, Joseph Swicket established a fair at Bradfield, and in the following year John Balguy started a Saturday market and four annual fairs in Hope. Before its Thursday market and three-day June fair were established in 1699, Penistone was just a small, hill-top village. A War Office enquiry into accommodation in 1686 found only five guest beds and three stables there and a local assessment of 1697 recorded no innkeepers and only a few tradesmen amongst the thirty-three householders. A petition in favour of the new market attracted 2,140 signatures from all the neighbouring villages and from as far away as Manchester, Stockport, Glossop, and Sheffield. The market place that was laid out in front of the church tower had an immediate impact upon the local economy. Inns and shops soon began to appear and the grammar school was revitalised. By 1770 Penistone had four annual fairs for horned cattle and horses. The livestock market continued to be held in the central streets until as late as 1910, when it was moved to the western edge of the town.

Another striking development was the foundation of Nonconformist chapels after the Toleration Act of 1689. The hamlets and farmsteads of the huge moorland parishes were ill-served by the Church of England, for their medieval churches often lay miles away. Religious dissent flourished in an environment where men and women cherished their independence. On 30 August 1694 Revd Robert Meeke, minister of Slaithwaite chapelry, visited Tintwistle, where he 'went to see a new chapel, which is built for a nonconformist … There are since the Toleration, many chapells builded'. That which Elkanah Rich erected in 1692 next to his hall at Bullhouse, 2 or 3 miles west of Penistone church, remains Independent to this day.

The chapel-of-ease that Godfrey and Bridget Bosville restored at Midhope in 1705 is Nonconformist in its building style though it remained attached to the Church of England. Chinley Chapel was opened in 1711 to serve a dissenting congregation that had been formed in the late seventeenth century by William Bagshawe, the Apostle of the Peak. Other dissenting chapels that eventually became Unitarian included those founded by William Ronksley at Fulwood in 1729 and at Underbank, near Stannington, by Thomas Marriott in 1743. The Quakers too were active in moorland communities. Their surviving meeting houses include one at Wooldale and another at High Flatts, both founded by the Jacksons, yeoman-clothiers of Totties and Wooldale halls.

Housing standards improved considerably during the seventeenth century as timber-frames were replaced by stone buildings or hidden from

Hallowes. The ancient parish of Dronfield contains a fine group of seventeenth- and early eighteenth-century houses that were built by prosperous lead smelters and merchants. Hallowes was erected in 1657 for Andrew Morewood, whose medieval ancestors had taken their surname from Moorwood Farm, high above the Rivelin Valley.

view behind stone walls and slate roofs. Probate inventories show that house interiors gradually became better furnished and the rooms more numerous. The gabled halls of the minor gentry and substantial yeomen, such as that built for Robert and Mary Glossop on Offerton Moor in 1658, were lit by mullioned and transomed windows. Other fine examples of mid seventeenth-century halls were erected in the chapelry of Bradfield for the Steads of Onesacre and the Greaves family of Hallfield, while in the neighbouring parish of Penistone the Wordsworths of Water Hall and the Riches of Bullhouse Hall built in matching style.

In north Derbyshire, the flourishing lead trade allowed smelters and merchants to invest their wealth in new houses. In Dronfield parish, for instance, Andrew Morewood erected a gabled hall at Hallowes in 1657, the Burtons built at Cartledge and Holmesfield, and by the early years of the eighteenth century the village of Dronfield had four substantial halls, each of them housing lead smelters and merchants. In the Peak District, the fashion for gabled roofs survived as late as 1727, when Thomas Slacke completed Slack Hall, near Chapel-en-le-Frith. Meanwhile, many a modest farmhouse was rebuilt in a simpler style. The early modern period was a time of increasing prosperity for the moorland communities.

The nickname Cakes of Bread was given to these rocks on Derwent Edge.

Chapter 5

Improvement and Enclosure

The great improvements to the transport system in the eighteenth and nineteenth centuries, first with the construction of turnpike roads then with the coming of the railways, made the Peak District accessible. Yet at the same time, the enclosure of huge tracts of moorland resulted in the creation of vast grouse-shooting estates and the exclusion of the public by hostile landowners and gamekeepers.

Turnpike roads

From the middle years of the eighteenth century onwards, as the national population soared and industry boomed, the parish repair system was no longer able to cope with the increasing amount of commercial traffic on the highways. This was the time too when summer visitors came in search of better health at the spa towns of Buxton and Matlock and to see the seven 'Wonders of the Peak' that lay mainly in the limestone district but which included Mam Tor and Chatsworth House on the edges of the gritstone moors.

The answer to the problem of poorly maintained roads was to form turnpike trusts, which were empowered by private Acts of Parliament to improve and maintain named stretches of important highways and to pay for this work by levying tolls on the users. The landowners and businessmen who formed these trusts were concerned with improving the major thoroughfares for 'the Benefit of Trade'. Meanwhile, the minor routes that connected the turnpike roads to villages, hamlets and farmsteads long remained the responsibility of the parish repair system, though some of the moorland tracks were widened and straightened by the various enclosure commissioners.

The first turnpike road in the Peak District (and the fiftieth in England) was that which wound its way from Manchester and Stockport to Whaley Bridge, from where travellers could continue via Buxton or Chapel-en-le-Frith. A petition presented to the House of Commons in 1724 claimed that this was 'the most direct Way from the Town of Manchester to the City of London; and is very deep and bad, and in some Parts so bad, that Coaches and Waggons cannot pass through the same with safety'. A few years later William Wright claimed that before local roads were turnpiked they were 'so bad in many Places, that they were almost impassable', but now they were fit for wheeled vehicles as well as for packhorses. However, he noted that on this particular highway 'the greatest part of the Toll has been raised by Horses, carrying Malt from Derby, and the parts adjacent into Cheshire; but Malt has, since the Road was in part repaired, been chiefly carried by Carts, drawn with Two Horses; which has very much lessened the Profit of the Toll'. In 1749 this turnpike road was extended over the White Peak to Hurdlow and so on to Ashbourne or Derby.

In 1735 the earliest turnpike trust in the West Riding took over the maintenance of the highway from Rochdale to Halifax over Blackstone Edge. Six years later, half-a-dozen new schemes improved the links between the industrial towns of Lancashire and Yorkshire. All the supporting petitions to Parliament emphasised the great amount of traffic on these ancient Pennine routes. The medieval saltway up the Cheshire panhandle, which had been turnpiked in 1732 as far as the county boundary at Saltersbrook, was improved in 1741 on the Yorkshire side of the border so as to connect with the Don Navigation at Rotherham and Doncaster.

A House of Commons committee found that 'great quantities of manufactured goods, cheese, salt, and potatoes, are carried from Manchester, Barnsley and parts adjacent, to Doncaster, on horses, and return loaded with hemp, flax, and German yarn' and that the trade could be carried on much easier in 'waggons, carts, etc'. The new bridge over Saltersbrook, which was just wide enough to take wheeled vehicles, remained in use until this crossing was abandoned in 1828 in favour of a wider bridge and a road diversion further upstream. A turnpike milestone on the original route beyond the ancient bridge reads: 'From Wortley XII Miles From Rotherham XXI Miles'. Thomas Jeffreys's map of Yorkshire, which was published in 1772, marks this stone and the next one, beyond the Lady Cross, which is inscribed simply XX. The original highway can still be followed further along the 'Snow Road' (which was so-called because its wooden posts marked the route in winter time) down to the former toll bar at Bordhill, where it was met by the 1828 diversion. Its course up the steep climb to Hartcliff and along the ridgeway towards Rotherham is still indicated by the XVI, XV and XIV milestones that are marked on Jeffreys's map, but it proved uneconomic and was abandoned as a commercial venture in 1788. Nevertheless, it continued in use as a local route and as a means of driving cattle the other way from Rotherham's famous livestock markets and fairs to the industrial towns of Lancashire and Cheshire. When the local moors were enclosed in the early nineteenth century the road was straightened and given a standard width between defining walls.

In 1758 the highway from Wakefield and Huddersfield across the moors to the county boundary at Austerlands and down to Manchester and Oldham was turnpiked. It followed the ancient route via Crossland Moor and Gate Head to Marsden and over the Standedge escarpment to Saddleworth. Its advocates described it as 'being situated in a trading and populous Part of the [West Riding], and much used and frequented for the carriage and Conveyance of Goods, Wares and Merchandize, Commodities and Provisions, made, manufactured and consumed in that Country ... from the Narrowness and Steepness thereof in many Places and the nature of the soil, [it has] become so deep and ruinous that in Winter and Wet-Seasons the same is almost impassable for Wheel Carriages ...'. Thomas Jeffreys's county map marked the fifteen milestones on the way from Huddersfield to

The bridge over Salters' Brook, the county boundary stream between Cheshire and Yorkshire, was built when the ancient highway was turnpiked between 1732 and 1741. In the background is the new bridge of 1828.

Austerlands, but in 1820 a new route was opened along the Colne Valley to Marsden via the growing industrial settlement of Slaithwaite.

In Derbyshire, in 1759, the moorland highway that went from Chesterfield to Curbar Gap, before descending steeply to Calver and climbing up through Stoney Middleton, Tideswell and Peak Forest, was turnpiked as far as Sparrowpit Gate, where it joined the main road to Manchester. An original milestone, set within a later wall when the enclosure commissioners gave the route a regular width, survives near Whibbersley Cross. It is inscribed 'Chesterfield 6 Miles; Tideswell 10, Manchester 36', and is similar in style to milestones that were erected in the previous year on Houndkirk Moor and Longshaw on the Sheffield to Buxton and Sparrowpit Gate turnpike road. This route out of Sheffield followed the medieval Psalter Lane to Banner Cross, Bents Green and Ringinglow, where a three-storeyed, octagonal toll house of 1795 stands where the road splits into two. One branch went straight ahead towards Callow Bank, Hathersage, Hope and Castleton, then up Winnats Pass to Sparrowpit Gate. The other turned left and headed across Houndkirk Moor to Fox House and through Longshaw to Grindleford Bridge, where it began the steep ascent of the Sir William Hill

The old highway across Houndkirk Moor provides a vivid impression of what an early moorland turnpike road looked like. It was embanked in this section and maintained in a rough-and-ready way from 1758, but was neglected after 1812 when a new turnpike road from Sheffield via Dore provided a better route to Longshaw. A milestone alongside this route notes the distance to Tideswell and Buxton.

and continued in a direct line along the ridge to Tideswell and Buxton. This route still gives a vivid impression of the nature of the early turnpike roads, which stuck rigidly to the line of the ancient highways across the moors. It was the longest of the primitive, poorly made turnpike roads that were improved later on by diversion and modification.

The Cat and Fiddle route over the moors from Macclesfield to Buxton was also turnpiked in 1759 and the improvement of the moorland highway from Buxton to Leek was begun six years later. The growing spa, market and industrial town of Buxton was now linked by turnpike roads in all directions: to Stockport, Macclesfield, Leek and Sheffield.

The aim of the early turnpike trusts was not to replace the ancient highways with new routes but to maintain and improve existing ones. The lack of adequate technology and of experienced road builders meant that the surveyors employed by the trustees had to be content with applying old methods of repair more thoroughly and regularly than before. They soon discovered that the best road surfaces were made with fired grit, chert and limestone gravel, or hard slag, and with large stones that were broken into smaller pieces. Drainage was a continual problem in boggy districts.

Proposals for new routes were often hindered by the opposition of landowners. John Farey, the author of the *General View of the Agriculture and Minerals of Derbyshire*, wrote in 1817 about the Sheffield to Buxton road:

> The tremendous descents into Monksdale valley and other scarcely less formidable, in the road between Tideswell and Buxton, might have been avoided and a very good line of Road adopted ... by passing through the village of Wheston, by Dale-head and Small-dale, but for the opposition of a Mr Robert Freeman, who then resided at Wheston, and did not like a Turnpike Road through his village! Egregious folly this, very common in the last age.

He also commented that:

> The early projectors and makers of the Turnpike Roads ... too closely imitated the defective system on which Roads had been previously set out; not only in unnecessarily ascending hills, where more level lines might have been chosen, but in descending directly into, and thus crossing valleys at right angles, instead of the more oblique and easy descents which might in most instances be had.

The first turnpike road that was designed with an easy gradient was that constructed in 1764 as a diversion from Whaley to Chapel-en-le-Frith and Sparrowpit Gate via Tunstead Milton and Barmoor Clough, in preference to the old route past Eccles Pike and Peaslow, which had gradients of up to one-in-four. In 1781 the route from Greenhill Moor (Norton) to Hathersage by Millstone Edge, and to Stoney Middleton by Froggatt Edge, had to be carefully engineered, but it was not until the turn of the century that the new technique of cutting terraces into hillsides was developed. A classic example of how an ancient moorland crossing with steep gradients was provided with only minor diversions and with bridges to take wheeled traffic is provided by the Strines route from Ladybower to Penistone, launched in 1771 by Hans Winthrop Mortimer, Lord of Bamford, MP, and owner of large estates in Essex, Derbyshire and London. Thomas Jeffreys marked it simply as a 'Bridleway' at the time when the improvements began.

Strines is a dialect word for a stream or a narrow river crossing, and the Strines Inn was built to cater for the new wheeled traffic along this ancient route. John Wilson, the antiquary of Broomhead Hall, noted in his journal in 1776: 'Anthony Worrall set up the sign of the Bull at Strynds and sold ale.' Opposite the inn is a stone inscribed 'Take Off' where an extra horse supplied by the innkeeper was detached after the climb from the new bridge that was built in 1775. A similar stone can be found in the roadside wall on the summit above Sheephouse Farm before Mortimer's Road descends to Penistone. This section, from Midhopestones to Cubley, was a new diversion that avoided the ancient direct route up past Judd Field Farm, though in parts the gradient was still one-in-four.

A dramatic new diversion through the Peak District was created in 1811 when the Winnats Pass, which ascends a limestone gorge near Castleton, was replaced by a road that wound its way up the slopes of Mam Tor and continued in a straight line below Rushup Edge to Chapel-en-le-Frith. In modern times this road has had to be closed because of serious subsidence. The first new route along a valley was the Wadsley to Langsett turnpike road of 1805, which provided a link between the highway from Sheffield to Halifax and the turnpike over Saltersbrook. It was extended beyond the Flouch Inn towards Huddersfield through Hazlehead and Crowedge in 1821.

The most ambitious of all the local turnpikes was Snake Pass, which was begun in 1818. This was a new highway that replaced an old route from Sheffield to Glossop, through Stannington and Lockerbrook and up Doctor's

Gate. It was opened in 1821 and acquired its popular name because halfway between Ashopton and Glossop the Duke of Devonshire built an inn, which was distinguished by the sign of the Cavendish snake. The new road crossed some of the wildest scenery in Derbyshire by skirting the northern side of Kinder Scout and climbing over Bleaklow.

Canals and railways

The Peak District moors were formidable obstacles to canal engineers, but an ingenious solution of linking the Cromford canal to the Peak Forest canal at Bugsworth was provided by the construction of the Cromford & High Peak Railway across some of the wildest parts of the White Peak between 1825 and 1831, with nine steep inclines worked by horses and steam engines. Even more dramatic was the boring of the Standedge tunnel through the Pennines so that narrowboats could transport goods along the Huddersfield canal to Ashton-under-Lyne.

Standedge Tunnel. This major feat of engineering took the Huddersfield Canal through the Pennines from Marsden to Diggle and on to Manchester. It was opened in 1811 and thrived until railway tunnels were bored alongside it. The canal basin and the tunnel were re-opened as a tourist attraction with a Visitor Centre in 2001.

A huge labour force of Irish navvies who lived in temporary settlements on the edge of the moors began work in 1794 under the direction of Benjamin Outram, but progress was slow and in 1805 Thomas Telford, the greatest canal engineer of his day, was called in to rectify mistakes in the alignment. When it was completed in 1811, the tunnel stretched 5,456 yards between Marsden and Diggle and was the longest, deepest and highest on any English canal. Much of the tunnel was lined with bricks, but some stretches were left as roughly faced rock, which made it difficult for the boatmen to 'leg' their way through. Journeys could take up to four hours. No tow paths were provided, so the horses were led over the hill, four times a day, seven days a week, by Thomas Bourne, who started this job at the age of 12 and continued at it for thirty-seven years. The canal declined when railway tunnels were bored alongside it in 1848, 1871 and 1894. The last one is still used by trains from Huddersfield to Manchester.

The most ambitious railway engineering project in the Peak District attracted national fame. This was the 3 miles and 13 yards long Woodhead tunnel, which linked Sheffield to Manchester by crossing the moors at about 1,000 feet above sea level. Work began in 1839 and took six years to complete. More than 1,500 navvies worked night and day, including Sundays, at twelve different rock faces, and all but 1,000 yards of the tunnel had to be lined with masonry to prevent falls from the roof. The ventilation shafts descended by as much as 579 feet. The work was arduous, unpleasant and dangerous, for the men often had to stand ankle-deep and sometimes knee-deep in mud and water, and if they tried to quench their thirst by drinking the water that streamed down the walls they suffered from chronic diarrhoea.

When he was questioned at a parliamentary enquiry in 1846, Wellington Purdon, the assistant engineer to Joseph Locke, agreed that perhaps a safety fuse was a better way of conducting explosions than the one he employed, but he argued that 'it is attended with such a loss of time, and the difference is so very small, I would not recommend the loss of time for the sake of all the extra loss of lives it would save'. The records are incomplete, but at least thirty-two men were killed while building the tunnel and twenty-three cases of compound fractures, seventy-four simple fractures, and 140 serious cases involving burns, lacerations and dislocations were reported. The Victorian reformer Edwin Chadwick observed that the three per cent killed and fourteen per cent wounded nearly equalled the proportionate casualties of a military campaign or a severe battle.

The navvies lived with their wives, mistresses and children in stone huts near the Yorkshire end of the tunnel at Dunford Bridge and in more primitive conditions at Woodhead. They were attracted to these lonely spots by high wages and when they were paid every quarter of the year many went on a drunken rampage, to the alarm of the respectable inhabitants of the towns and villages a few miles away. When a second bore was constructed alongside the original tunnel between 1847 and 1852 working conditions were better and fewer men died, though an outbreak of cholera killed twenty-eight navvies at Woodhead in 1849.

In 1894 an alternative route from Sheffield to Manchester via the Hope Valley and New Mills was opened. The formidable engineering problems along this line included a tunnel that was 3 miles 950 yards long between Totley and Grindleford and the 3,702-yard long Cowburn tunnel between Edale and Chinley. Bulmer's *Directory* (1895) noted that: 'by the construction of this line, the wild and romantic scenery of Peakland is thrown open to the admiring gaze of visitors and tourists'. This was the railway line that the Sheffield Clarion Ramblers used to get to Edale on their first organised walk in 1900.

Farming before enclosure

In the second volume of his *General View of the Agriculture and Minerals of Derbyshire* (1813), John Farey wrote that:

The High Moors … are distinguished into black and white Lands, the former being by far the most extensive, and are uniformly covered by Heath, which at a distance appears of a dark brown, approaching to black, of a most dismal aspect; the latter are the better and green parts, where Grasses prevail instead of Heath, or the aquatics on the very wet peaty parts called Mosses, which are still more dreary in their appearance than the black Heaths … Lowk Grass, a kind of fine Benty Grass, occupying the wetter parts of the Moors, is found more productive of keep than the coarse Bents that occupy some other parts, among the Heath, Ling, and Bilberry Plants … Bilberry stems, Black Whorts, Wortleberry, or Huckleberry, … are the next most prevailing Herbage on the Moors, after and among the Heaths, especially where short Heath is alone seen, and which parts are generally found the most difficult to improve. Moors much abounding with Bilberry wyzles or stems are very unproductive of sheep, and won't summer, or carry much more than half a Sheep to an acre, exclusive of the improved valleys. The Bilberry, a small black Fruit, is gathered by the Poor, and used for Puddings and Pies, and it is also served up in Desserts at the Tables of the more wealthy, in the vicinity of the Moor Lands.

Four years later, Farey also wrote about a breed of sheep that was particularly suited to grazing on the moors: 'Woodland or Moorland Sheep are rather a small and long-legged sort of horned Sheep, whose wool is fine, except on the breech, in general these Sheep have white faces, but some have black specks on their noses and legs.' He provided a list of 'Woodland Sheep-breeders in Derbyshire' and noted that two Shepherds' Societies met at Hayfield and Saltersbrook to agree on a marking system so that strays could be reported. In south-west Yorkshire the 'Whitefaced Woodlands' breed was known as the Penistone.

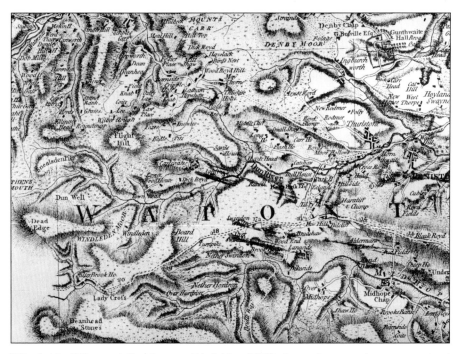

This detail of Thomas Jeffreys' map of Yorkshire (1772) shows the extensive moors around Penistone a few decades before a series of enclosure Acts transformed the landscape. The hachuring depicts the extent of the moors in contrast to the blank spaces, which were cultivated.

In their *General View of the Agriculture of the West Riding of Yorkshire* (1793) the Board of Agriculture reporters, Rennie, Brown and Shirreff, observed that:

> The sheep bred upon the moors in the western parts of the Riding, and which, we presume, are the native breed, are horned, light in the fore quarter, and well made for exploring a hilly country, where there is little to feed them, but heath and ling; these are generally called the Peniston breed, from the name of the market town, where they are sold. When fat they will weigh from 10 [pounds] to 15 [pounds] per quarter. They are a hardy kind of sheep, and good thrivers. When brought down, at a proper age, to the pastures in the low parts of the country, they feed as cleverly, and are as rich mutton as needs be … Those breeds above Peniston are well adapted to those uncultivated barren mountains.

An earlier *General View of the Agriculture of Derbyshire* by T. Brown in 1794 had observed that in the Peak District (including the limestone plateau): 'About one fifth of the enclosures may be arable, and this fifth part chiefly employed in growing oats; the remainder is in pasture, and the greatest part employed in dairying and breeding of stock.'

A notable feature of the sixth edition of William Owen's *Book of Fairs* (1770) was the listing of new livestock fairs on the edges of the moors. Although the market that had been founded at Hope in 1715 was defunct cattle fairs were held there every May Day and at Michaelmas. Matlock had four fairs for horned cattle and sheep and Darley Flash was the venue for twice-yearly fairs for sheep and cattle. Across the Yorkshire border, Bradfield held two fairs a year, mainly for swine, Holmfirth had a 30 October fair for horned cattle, and Penistone's Thursday market and seasonal fairs continued to flourish.

These reports are informative about the state of farming just before the parliamentary enclosure of the moorlands. In 1793 Rennie, Brown and Shirreff noted that the climate of Penistone parish was 'cold and backward to vegetation', the soil 'very variable, but mostly wet and spongy, and a great deal of moor carrying little but heath'. Off the moors the farms were small and 'Mr Bosville of Gunthwaite' was the only large owner. About half the land around the small market town was ploughed, but much of the extensive parish consisted of moorland. Oats and a small quantity of wheat were the only cereals, and both seed time and harvesting were late. Indeed, the harvest was sometimes not gathered until November.

This description is supported by comments in the various crop returns that were requested by the government in 1801 at the time of the Napoleonic wars. The curate wrote: 'Tho' the parish of Penistone is very extensive, yet there is little land upon the Plow in Comparison, the Farms in general being grazing and Stock farms.' Another curate observed that: 'The Chapelry of Bradfield is more proper for breeding sheep and other cattle than growing corn,' and the curate of Bolsterstone and Midhope reported that: 'As we lie in the highest and coldest part between Liverpool and Hull, the quantity of wheat grown on an Acre here will not average more than 18 Bushels, Oats 4 Quarters, and Barley 3½ Quarters. ... Yet I can assure you that forty years ago, there was not one tenth part of the wheat grown in this place that is grown at present; nor one half of the Peas or Barley. NB. all the inhabitants live wholly on Oat Bread and use no wheat, but for Pies and Puddings.'

In his *Tour of the Don* (1837), John Holland was impressed by the tasty oatcakes when he visited the Rose and Crown Inn that William Payne, lord of the manor of Langsett, had built in 1802: 'When a person enters the inn, at which the coaches stop at Midhope Stones, the first thing that strikes his eyes, especially if he is hungry, is a sort of rack suspended on the joists of the ceiling of the kitchen, and overlaid with some scores of thin oat-cakes, or, as the batch is called, reed bread; having been placed on the rails of the rack in its flaccid state, the manner in which each cake is warped, first by hanging over at the edges, and secondly by drying, gives it a curious appearance to a stranger. When eaten, it is found to be just so tenderly crisp, and withal so sweet, added to its undoubted wholesomeness, that many persons are extremely fond of it.'

Boundaries before enclosure

Until the enclosure awards of the late eighteenth and early nineteenth centuries divided the commons and wastes and compelled the new owners to construct drystone walls around their properties, the boundaries between the grazing and peat digging zones belonging to different parishes and townships were often vague and disputed. Streams and prominent rocks formed natural divisions, but on the open moors the placing of boundary stones and crosses caused much wrangling.

At Rogationtide (the Monday, Tuesday and Wednesday before Ascension Day) it was the custom in many parts of England for parishioners to 'beat' or 'perambulate' their bounds, with a reading from the Gospels at certain points and amusing pranks at others, such as turning the vicar upside down and threatening to drop him into a well, so that these boundary markers would remain in young people's memories. As it was difficult to walk round the lengthy boundaries of the extensive Peak District parishes, even if a few days were set aside to complete the task, Rogationtide processions across the moors were not undertaken regularly. Instead, the accounts that survive in manor court rolls or parish chests suggest that moorland perambulations were arranged in the summer months on specific occasions in order to settle claims about township or manorial boundaries.

One such record, which can be followed on the ground today, was made by John Barker, the Duke of Rutland's steward, when the freeholders and tenants of Holmesfield perambulated their bounds on 25 August 1777:

- Beginning at Moor Woodnook up a Sick to its rise from thence to a Stone on the Top of Brownedge Markt H. This appears to be an Antient Boundary Mark, and so far I believe is right.
- From thence in a strait Line West over Totley Moss to a Wooden Pole at the end of Totley Moss which stands in a Stone markt TW. This was claimed by Totley people as the Boundary Mark betwixt them and Hathersage and I believe it to be so.
- From thence going South to Lady's Cross, we found a Stone on the Black Hill markt TW which the Totley people said was their Boundary Mark.
- From Lady's Cross we went down Deadshaw to Barbrook. The Holmesfield people said there had been a mark H on a stone on the Top of Deadshaw Sick and another on the Bottom of Deadshaw Sick, but none was seen there.
- We went down Barbrook to Black Brook and up Black brook to Lease Fenn where a Stone stood marked H which had been that day turned over and endeavoured to be buried in Leas fen supposed to be done by some Barlow people seen near it.
- From this stone in a Line to Holmesfield Inclosures.
- NB. I shou'd suppose from consideration of the above Boundary and from the Baslow Boundary and other observations that the real Boundary of Holmesfield shou'd be as under or nearly so, Viz:
- From Moor Wood Nook to the Stone on the Top of Brownedge, and from thence in a straight Line to the Totley Mark on Black hill TW. From thence to the Hurkling Stone and then to Ladys Cross and then to Stone Bridge and down Barbrook as above.

The Hurkling Stone, Big Moor. Hurkling was an old dialect word for 'crouching' that was often applied to large rocks that appeared to squat on the skyline. This one acted as a natural boundary marker. The deeply incised 'MB' with a cross signified the manor of Baslow. In the centre is a T for Totley and out of sight is an H for Holmesfield.

The inhabitants of Baslow perambulated their bounds at the same time, starting at Whibbersley Cross and heading over Leash Fen to Black Brook. They recorded several stones marked with a cross and the letters MB for the manor of Baslow, such as when they 'proceeded up Barbrook to a place where the Horse Road from Curbar to Holmesfield Crossed the said Brook and there Orders were given to set the Letters MB with a Cross under upon a Stone at the west side of the said Brook'. They found similar marks on the Hurkling Stone and the Lady Cross before heading for Windley Well.

Meanwhile, the men and youths of Barlow were also out recording their boundaries. The three parties met at Leash Fen. It seems that the officers of the Duke of Rutland, who was lord of the manor of all three townships, had determined to resolve disputes by this concerted activity rather than let them be settled with the use of force, as had happened on the Thurlstone and Holmfirth moors in the early sixteenth century.

Parliamentary enclosure

Some former moors close to towns and villages are now known only by their place-names, for they were soon built upon to provide housing for the expanding population. Sheffield, for example, has a central street known simply as The Moor, which was the common of the inhabitants of Little Sheffield. During the second half of the eighteenth century and the first half of the nineteenth, millions of acres of commons, wastes and open fields in England and Wales were enclosed by thousands of private Acts of Parliament. In the parish of Sheffield the Ecclesall commons and wastes that were enclosed between 1779 and 1788 included 268 acres of high moors beyond Ringinglow and several greens. Then the commons and wastes of the townships and hamlets of Upper Hallam, Nether Hallam, Stannington, Storrs and Dungworth were enclosed between 1791 and 1805. The proposal for this enclosure, which was put forward in 1787 by the Duke of Norfolk (the lord of the manor) and other landowners, met with opposition from 'several of the freeholders and inhabitants', but these opponents owned insufficient land to resist.

The enclosure of the Black Moors of the former Rivelin Chase was not contentious, for these were ancient private lands, but the loss of Crookesmoor and its racecourse, on the edge of Sheffield, aroused hostility. When the process of enclosure at Crookesmoor began in 1791 the surveyors were met

Gorse in full bloom on unused land at Pudding Pie Hill, west of Chesterfield, gives a sense of the appearance of moorland edges before the improvements associated with parliamentary enclosure. The alternative names of broom and whin are preserved in minor place-names such as Broomhead (Yorkshire) or Win Hill (Derbyshire).

by an angry crowd and the authorities had to call for armed forces to restore order.

As we have seen, some of the Peak District moors had been divided up in the late seventeenth and early eighteenth centuries, long before the period of parliamentary enclosure. John Farey estimated that about half the Derbyshire moors were private, notably the Duke of Devonshire's Hope Woodlands and Lord Howard's lordship of Glossop. On the Yorkshire side of the Upper Derwent Valley the Duke of Norfolk's tenants rented farms whose pastures and sheepwalks had been defined centuries earlier by earthen banks. There were no commons and wastes in that part of Hallamshire to include in the Bradfield enclosure award.

The popular view that everyone had rights on the commons is mistaken. Only that minority of the inhabitants who were landowners possessed common rights and these varied in proportion to the size of their farms. They were the ones who received allotments in lieu of their former rights upon the publication of an enclosure award. The commissioners' first job was to listen to claims and to establish who were legally entitled to recompense. In the Rivelin Valley the inhabitants of Hallam, Fulwood, Stannington and Moorwood were allotted land in lieu of their ancient grazing rights, but seventy other people, including thirty-five cutlers and eighteen grinders, had their claims for compensation dismissed. Mr Gibson, acting on their behalf, asserted that 1,000 acres on the Black Moors were 'Rocks where the Poor burn Fearne and raise £120 by the Ashes'. He also claimed that the poor kept flocks of geese and 'many Galloways for Grinders to carry goods', but their case was dismissed by Mr Wood, whose legal opinion was sought by the enclosure commissioners, as being 'most of them Wheelfellows – probably many not Inhabitants'. He concluded that the late thirteenth-century charter allowed grazing rights only to the inhabitants who were freeholders, and that the grazing of geese and galloways and the burning of ashes were illegal practices that had arisen under lax manorial control after the removal of the deer from the chase when cutlers' grinding wheels were installed in the Rivelin Valley as trade and population increased.

The enclosure award allotted 7,232 acres of moorland and commons, including 3,935 acres in the township of Upper Hallam and 2,004 acres in Stannington. The Duke of Norfolk received the major share because of his ownership of Rivelin Chase and in lieu of the great and small tithes, which Francis, fifth Earl of Shrewsbury, had purchased upon the dissolution of the monasteries.

Enclosures below Stanage. These fields at Overstones Farm were created upon the enclosure of the commons and wastes of Hathersage in the early nineteenth century. Some of these pastures remain a vivid green colour within the patterns of walls that were first drawn up on a surveyor's drawing board, but others have reverted to moorland or are increasingly covered by rushes.

William Fairbank's map of the parish of Sheffield (1795) shows that some of the new allotments were marked out long before the publication of the enclosure award. Parts of Hallam Moor and Lodge Moor, for instance, were already divided into the large, rectangular fields that can still be recognised on the map and on the ground, though some have since been sub-divided and others have reverted to moorland. One of these fields was named Rape Piece because rapeseed was the first crop to be grown there, followed by black oats, turnips and potatoes. But soon all these new enclosures were used solely for grazing.

Large stretches of moorland were brought into cultivation for the first time upon the completion of the enclosure process. The new green pastures now provide a vivid contrast to the surviving moorlands immediately beyond. Among the many striking new fields that were created from the Eastern Moors in this way are those at Stoke Flat, Curbar Gap and Upper Loads, but examples can be found throughout the Peak District. In the twentieth century, some of these new enclosures, particularly those above Darley Dale and Matlock, were converted into conifer plantations while others were abandoned to soft rushes and thistles. The improvers were frequently over-optimistic about what could be achieved.

The Bolsterstone enclosure award of 1782 is an early example that dealt with nearly 3,000 acres of Nether Commons, Upper Commons and Whitwell Moor. Lord Melbourne owned 1,984 acres and, as lord of the manor, was entitled to all the minerals, coal delphs and stone quarries. The commissioners concluded that 1,240 acres on Upper Commons were: 'so bad in nature as in our opinion they will not at present answer the expenses of fencing and inclosing. Therefore we do allot the same to be an open pasture for the use of the said Lord Melbourne only.' In all, Lord Melbourne was allotted 1,544 acres, the owners of the tithes received 386 acres, the twenty-seven freeholders got 198 acres between them, and other small allotments amounted to 34 acres.

Most of the local moors were enclosed by numerous private Acts of Parliament during the first half of the nineteenth century. For instance, between 1800 and 1826 the extensive commons and wastes of Penistone parish were enclosed by six private Acts and Awards: Ingbirchworth (1800–13), Hunshelf (1810–13), Langsett (1811–14), Thurlstone (1812–16), Oxspring (1818–26) and Penistone (1819–26). Where the wastes were large and the boundaries complicated, the commissioners and their surveyors spent years in sorting out the rival claims. The owners of the new allotments then employed labourers to build the drystone field walls that are now such a characteristic feature of the Peak District and to lay out long, straight lanes, some of which were entirely new while others were ancient routes that were straightened and given standard widths of 40 feet for the highways and 30 feet or less for the byways.

Thomas Jeffreys' map of Yorkshire, published in 1772 before enclosure, shows how little of Penistone parish had been cultivated in comparison with the huge amount of unfenced common grazing. Thurlstone township, for example, contained 8,116 acres, of which 6,522 were commons and wastes. Within a generation, the landscape of Penistone parish was transformed by all this activity.

In 1802 William Payne of Frickley Hall, north-west of Doncaster, had bought Lord Melbourne's 925-acre estate in Langsett, with 'an unlimited right of Pasturage upon Langsett Common and Moor, which are very extensive and from which considerable improvements are expected upon an Inclosure'. The advertisement for the sale claimed that 'The Estate is capable of great Improvement which has been much neglected owing to its great distance from the proprietor'. The enclosure award of 1814 allotted 2,547 acres to Payne, including the whole 2,045 acres of the rough High Moors. Four years later, he sold the estate at a profit.

The other wastes in Langsett township – Penistone Common (298 acres), Fullshaw Common (243), Long Moor (146), Bordhill Common (123), Swinden Common (113) and smaller commons at Langsett Bank, Paw Hill and Swinden Walls – included much land that could be improved, so new rectangular fields were soon divided by stone walls that followed the straight lines drawn on the surveyors' maps. Payne was responsible for some interesting experiments in the design of the new walls to provide shelter for his sheep whichever way the wind was blowing and the rain or snow was falling. In his *Tour of the Don* (1837) John Holland wrote:

> The situation of Penistone is peculiarly bleak and exposed; and the cultivated tract by which the town is surrounded, was formerly remarkable, not more for the paucity of its produce, than for the lateness of the period at which the crops commonly yielded to the influence of the gentler seasons. Of late years, the agricultural aspect of the neighbourhood appears to have undergone a striking change for the better.

The 3,332 acres of commons and wastes in the neighbouring manor of Midhope were enclosed between 1818 and 1823. Godfrey Bosville of Gunthwaite Hall at the northern edge of Penistone parish, whose ancestor and namesake had bought the manor of Midhope in the late seventeenth century, received the largest share. Indeed, a section of the Midhope grouse moor is known as Bosville's Piece to this day. Other landowners who came from even further away included William Payne and Marmaduke Middleton, Esq, of Leam Hall, Derbyshire. The rest of the chapelry of Bradfield was enclosed in 1811–26, when the Duke of Norfolk, lord of the manor, was awarded about half of the 13,773 acres of commons and wastes, most of it rough moorland suitable only for grazing sheep and shooting grouse. The duke already owned about 4 square miles of 'Holden Heys, Little Holden and Holden Pasture', that is the cattle heys and sheep walks attached to his farms at Howden a previous lord had purchased at the dissolution of the monasteries. Earl Fitzwilliam of Wentworth Woodhouse was awarded 741 acres on Thornseat Moor and 23 acres in Hall Field, to which he soon added by purchase 736 acres to the east of Foulstone Delf. It remains in the possession of the Wentworth estate to this day. The Rimington-Wilsons of Broomhead Hall also got about 300 acres and they began to create what in time would become the famous grouse moor at Broomhead by the gradual purchase of another 925 acres.

Rough, unimprovable moors such as these were quickly adapted to the shooting of grouse. As we have seen, the Duke of Rutland built Longshaw Lodge as the centre of his sporting estate after he had acquired a huge stretch of the Eastern Moors upon the enclosure of the commons and wastes of Hathersage (1808–30), Holmesfield (1816–20), Baslow (1819–26), Barlow (1817–29), Brampton (1815–31), Dore (1809–22) and Totley (1839–42). Further north, on 13 June 1829 the *Leeds Chronicle* advertised the auction of nearly 2,800 acres of moorland enclosed within the Graveship of Holme, which were bound by other sporting estates, including the Spencer-Stanhope moors at Dunford. The advertisement noted that these were 'worthy of the attention of sportsmen, being excellent moors, well-stocked with grouse'. This was just a portion of the 9,200 acres of commons and wastes within the graveship that were enclosed between 1828 and 1834. Unusually, 40 of these acres, in five separate allotments, were placed in trust under the Constable of the Graveship of Holme 'for the benefit of the owners and Proprietors … and their Tenants and Occupiers of Estates situate within the said Graveship for the purpose of their digging and getting Peats or Turves therein to be used and consumed in their respective dwelling houses within the said Graveship but not to be sold given way or otherwise used applied or disposed of '. They remain under the constable's supervision and they have been used occasionally in modern times, such as the national fuel shortage of 1947 or the coal miners' strikes of the 1970s and 1980s.

The Lord of the Graveship of Holme was the Duke of Leeds, whereas at neighbouring Meltham, which was enclosed between 1817 and 1832, the lordship was divided between six people, four of whom were local men. The township had 3,645 acres of commons and wastes compared with only 1,004 acres that were already farmed. The 1801 crop returns show that only 160 acres were cultivated in Meltham, with 145 acres of oats, 10 acres of wheat, 2 acres of barley, 2 acres of potatoes, and 1 acre of turnips. Further west the 7,220 acres of Saddleworth's commons and wastes were enclosed between 1830 and 1834.

Meanwhile, in Staffordshire the pressure on the commons was beginning to tell in the years leading up to enclosure. The 310 acres of Longsdon Moor and the 280 acres of Ladderedge had been enclosed in 1815, after which the

The Peacock Inn, Owler Bar, takes its name from the heraldic device of the Duke of Rutland, who acquired a vast moorland estate upon the parliamentary enclosure of the moors. The window styles are typical of the Haddon Estate buildings of that time. A toll bar by the inn collected tolls from four directions.

new allotments were limed and sown with grain and turnips. Three years later, a meeting of thirty-two inhabitants of Alstonefield township appointed five of their number to take proceedings against outsiders who were trespassing on the commons with their livestock and against inhabitants who were exceeding their pasture rights. The remaining 3,000 acres of wastes and open fields in the manor of Alstonefield – including the 940 acres of Morridge – were enclosed in 1839. Sir George Crewe of Calke Abbey, lord of the manor, acknowledged the 'loss of the wild and picturesque character which the country formerly bore', but he felt that enclosure was necessary to feed the rising population: 'no land which is capable of being cultivated can be allowed to idle for gratification to the eye.' He found that the cost of enclosure and of repairing farmhouses was heavy.

Victorian moorland halls, farmsteads and new settlements

The Harpur family of Calke Abbey changed their name to Crewe in 1808 and after 1844 used the form Harpur Crewe, which they altered to Harpur-Crewe in 1911. Before the early nineteenth century the Harpurs had rarely visited their Staffordshire Moorlands estate, but when Sir George Crewe, a young Evangelical with a strong sense of social responsibility, succeeded his father all this changed. He remarked later that he was probably the first head of his family who ever set foot there 'for any other purpose than shooting game'. He praised 'the bracing effect of the mountain air', became very interested in the area, and in 1830 built Warslow Hall for his agent and as a place to stay on visits. He was concerned to find, however, that his tenants were '100 years behind the rest of the world, well disposed but ignorant and simple-minded', and that conditions were particularly bad at Flash.

Improved communications and a general acceptance of the new mood of Romanticism about the moorlands encouraged landowners and businessmen to build substantial halls or lodges as moorland retreats. When Philip Brocklehurst inherited the Swythamley estate, originally a grange of Dieulacres Abbey, from his Uncle William in 1859 at the age of 21 he used his inherited wealth from a Macclesfield silk mill to build a substantial mansion and lay out grounds that were considered to be fit to receive royalty. He improved his farms, he enjoyed the hunting, shooting and fishing, and he wrote about the history, lore and customs of the neighbourhood. He remained at Swythamley until his death in 1904.

Likewise in the chapelry of Bradfield, on the other side of the Pennines, the seventeenth-century Broomhead Hall of the Wilson family was pulled down in 1831 and replaced by a new residence on the very edge of the moors, with several features that were fashionable at the time, both in plan and ornament. The new owner was James Rimington, esquire, the nephew and heir of the childless Henry Wilson. The next generation changed their name to Rimington-Wilson.

In the late nineteenth century another branch of the family, headed by Charles Macro-Wilson, built Waldershaigh on a remote site near Bolsterstone. In the same district, in 1927, Charles Boot of Sugworth Hall, the son and heir of Henry Boot, the founder of the construction firm of

By the nineteenth century, what had once been viewed with horror by travellers was seen as sublime. In 1860 a path was constructed 'along the whole length of the Roaches, on nearly the highest ridge, which can easily be travelled by a mule or a pony, and which often leads a pleasant excursion to explorers'.

that name, employed some of his workmen at the time of trade depression to construct a tower high above Bradfield Dale, using features from two old farmhouses nearby. Boot's Folly remains a striking feature in the local landscape.

Many new farmsteads and field barns were erected on the moorland edges after enclosure. In the Yorkshire part of the Peak District a typical farmstead consisted of a dwelling house and a barn built on a long axis under the same roof. The house part usually provided two-up two-down accommodation with a central chimney stack and a separate entrance. Unlike the medieval longhouses, very few of these farmhouses have internal communication between the domestic and farm sections, and their most prominent external feature is the high, arched entry which allowed a loaded hay cart or sledge to enter the barn. All these buildings were constructed of local stone and were given a stone-slate roof. They are known to students of vernacular architecture as laithe-houses (from the northern word for a barn, derived from Old Norse), and they are unique amongst English buildings in remaining unchanged in style over nearly 250 years. The earliest examples date from *c*.1650, but most were erected between the enclosure of the wastes and the late Victorian period. Many of them were occupied by smallholders who pursued traditional dual occupations, such as that of weaver-farmer.

Parliamentary enclosure of the commons in an urban setting was often prompted not by thoughts of agricultural improvement but by making land on the edges of towns available for building. When Little Sheffield Moor was enclosed in 1788 it was immediately built upon, as William Fairbank's 1797 map of Sheffield reveals. In the countryside too new industrial settlements grew up around former greens and commons. Millhouse Green in the parish of Penistone took its name from a fulling mill that was erected on the River Don during the reign of Queen Elizabeth I. Thomas Jeffreys's map of Yorkshire (1772) marks a house and the mill but shows no other buildings on this small piece of common grazing land. The green was enclosed in 1816 under the terms of the Thurlstone award and by Victorian times a new community of wiredrawers, umbrella makers, coal miners and miscellaneous other workers and their families had been formed there.

A few miles to the south, part of the moorland valley of the Little Don was converted into a thriving industrial town at Stocksbridge, which took its name from a small bridge over the Little Don that was erected by a member of the Stocks family, possibly the John Stocks who was recorded in 1716 and who had a fulling mill close by. A four-storey cotton mill that was erected in 1794–5 alongside the old mill was the first sign of things to come, though the mill itself did not last long. Ten years later a turnpike road was constructed along the valley, and soon afterwards the surrounding hills and moors were enclosed. Samuel Fox saw the potential of the site. His original business was that of wiredrawer and maker of huckles and gill-pins for woolcombers, but he soon turned to making umbrellas as well, and from 1854 he made his own crucible steel. The great leap forward was made eight years later when he began to convert steel by the new Bessemer process for the mass production of railway materials. Stocksbridge became a steel town and immigrants poured into the valley to live and work there. The 1881 census recorded 4,600 of them in 895 houses.

The most remarkable new community in the Staffordshire Moorlands was at Flash, which had grown from a tiny moorland settlement on the road from Leek to Buxton into the highest village in England, at 1,526 feet above sea level. A church was built there in 1744 and a Wesleyan chapel forty years later. In a parliamentary debate in 1786 it was claimed that Alstonefield parish (which included Flash) contained about 400 hawkers and pedlars, who had converted 'a barren and wild spot to a rich and fertile circuit'. By 1817 Flash had three inns and three shops and numerous cottages whose menfolk worked as pedlars and hawkers, selling silk ribbons from Leek, buttons from Macclesfield, and smallwares from Manchester, while the women and girls made more buttons for sale.

When Sir George Crewe first visited the district in 1819 or 1820, he thought he had reached 'the very end of the civilized world'. Flash village appeared to him as a dirty place that 'bore marks principally of Poverty, Sloth, and Ignorance'. In his book, *Smythamley and its Neighbourhood* (1874), Philip Brocklehurst described Flash as:

a wild and barren place – heath, stone walls and black commons meet the eye on every side, and there is scarcely a tree to be seen for miles

Flash Wesleyan Chapel. In 1784 a Methodist society of some sixty members erected a chapel at Flash, the highest village in England. This was rebuilt in its present form in 1821. The evening congregation at the time of the 1851 ecclesiastical census numbered 180. The chapel was closed in 1974 and converted into a house.

… The cottages on these dreary moors are generally as ugly and as low as possible, and seem hugging the ground to avoid the winds. Still you will generally find a white apron, a clean floor, with a bright fire and smiling face in most of them. Sufficiently near the top of these great hills, stands strange little Flash. There are in it a number of stone houses, very grim, but built so as to be as cold-tight as possible.

In the mid-1860s William Beresford observed that: 'A considerable number of coalpits exist in this vicinity; and all of them lie within a few miles of Flash … The coal is generally small, and not of the best quality.' The coal face was reached by 'levels, driven horizontally into the hillsides, so that the coal can be brought out on small tramways'. On the edges of the moors on both sides of the Pennines numerous small drift mines such as these obtained coal and sometimes gannister until the middle decades of the twentieth century. Elsewhere, the coming of the railways opened up distant markets for building stones and for the flags that paved the streets of the nation's towns and cities. Large quarries were dug on the enclosed moorlands and numerous small houses and cottages were erected on the fringes of the moors for the quarrymen and other industrial workers.

Reservoirs

Modern man's impact on the moorland landscape is marked particularly by the construction of reservoirs, most of which add to the beauty of the scenery, except where they are surrounded by monotonous straight rows of conifers climbing up their banks. During the late eighteenth and early nineteenth centuries the natural springs and wells could no longer meet the demand of the rapidly growing population for drinking water and the rivers had to be dammed to provide power for the textile mills. The deep valleys of the Pennines, where the annual rainfall was the highest in England except for the Lake District fells, were an obvious choice for the construction of large impounding reservoirs, which could provide a regular supply of piped water to distant places. A series of private Acts of Parliament authorised the flooding of valleys and the destruction of hamlets and farmsteads to make way for them.

The three Wessenden reservoirs south of Marsden were completed by a group of mill owners in 1800. In the Holme Valley in 1837 an Act authorised the construction of reservoirs at Bilberry, Holme Styes and Boshaw Whams.

That at Bilberry was built with insufficient strength, and on 5 February 1852, after prolonged heavy rainfall, water poured out of it when the huge embankment burst. The flood waters that swept down the narrow valley reached Holmfirth, 3 miles away, in about twenty minutes. Eighty-one people died that night, mostly in Hinchliffe Mill and Holmfirth. The buildings that were completely destroyed included four mills, ten dyehouses, three drying stoves, twenty-seven cottages, seven tradesmen's houses, seven shops, seven bridges, ten warehouses and eight barns and stables. Many more buildings were severely damaged and over 7,000 people were put out of work.

In Sheffield, Joseph Matthewman began to build reservoirs at Crookesmoor in 1782 to provide the townspeople with drinking water. Within fifty years a series of six large dams and four smaller ones had been constructed there to supply piped water to all parts of the town. The newly incorporated Sheffield Waterworks Company then built a storage reservoir at Redmires on Stanage Moor, from where water flowed by gravitation along a conduit to the Crookesmoor dams. The Lower Redmires reservoir was finished in 1849, the Upper in 1854.

Between 1830 and 1854 the Sheffield Waterworks Company constructed this long, curving conduit across Hallam Moors, leading into one of the three reservoirs at Redmires. They also built two reservoirs in the Rivelin Valley and brought drinking water by further conduits to Crookes, from where it was piped into the town.

An Act of 1853 authorised the company to build further reservoirs in the Loxley Valley. The imperfect construction of their first attempt with the Dale Dyke reservoir wreaked havoc on the night of 11 March 1864, when the embankment collapsed and 114 million cubic feet of water poured down the Don Valley towards Sheffield. Within forty minutes the dam was almost empty and 240 people and 693 animals were drowned. That night about 100 buildings and fifteen bridges were destroyed, and approximately 4,000 houses were damaged in the worst natural disaster that Britain had experienced by that time. The Dale Dyke reservoir was rebuilt in the 1870s and new reservoirs were constructed nearby at Agden (1871) and Strines (1875). Sheffield Corporation bought out the Waterworks Company in 1888, but did not build any more reservoirs until the prospect of neighbouring water authorities taking the resources of the local rivers prompted them to enter partnerships.

One of the most spectacular transformations of the moorland landscape occurred in the upper reaches of the River Derwent. In 1899 the Derwent Valley Water Board was created by the joint authorities of Leicester, Derby, Nottingham and Sheffield to construct huge reservoirs on the Derbyshire-Yorkshire border. Between 1901 and 1916 farmsteads and hamlets were submerged under the Howden and Derwent dams. At Millstone Edge the ancient quarry was extended along the skyline to Bole Hill and workshops and sheds were provided for 350–450 workers.

After the heaps of debris that had been left by the millstone makers had been removed, a hydraulic ram was installed to pump 12,000 gallons of water a day from a stream below. Steam-powered cranes hoisted the newly cut stones into trucks at loading bays, which took them by rail to a steep incline where they were lowered by cables connected to a self-winding drum to the new Sheffield-Manchester railway at Grindleford. The weight of each full truck forced an empty one back up the incline. Over 1.2 million tons of stone were sent from Bole Hill Quarry to the construction sites in the Derwent Valley during the 7½ years of this operation.

In 1908 the Derwent Valley Water Board employed 2,753 navvies on the Howden and Derwent dams. Many found lodgings in the nearby villages of Bamford, Bradwell, Castleton and Hope, but others were housed in temporary accommodation that was built by the Water Board in 1901–3 mid-way between the two reservoirs. This village was known officially as Birchinlee after a local farm, but it quickly acquired the nickname of Tin Town. Its three streets contained a school, a recreation hall, two hospitals, a bathhouse, a public house and a few shops. By August 1909, a total of 967 men, women and children, were housed there, mostly in plain, corrugated iron huts, which were lined inside with wood for insulation. These huts were removed when the reservoirs were completed, fourteen years after this huge project began.

Work commenced on the neighbouring reservoir at Ladybower in 1935 and continued without interruption during the Second World War. It was partly complete by February 1944, in time to be used for practice by the crews of the Dambusters who destroyed German reservoirs, and it was formally opened on 25 September 1945. Many of the residents of the village of Ashopton, whose homes had been demolished, were re-housed alongside water board employees in a new estate at Yorkshire Bridge.

The other massive scheme was that begun by Manchester Corporation in the Longdendale Valley in 1848. In the next thirty years, reservoirs were completed at Arnfield and Hollingworth (1854), Rhodeswood (1855), Torside (1864), Vale House (1869) and Bottoms and Woodhead (1877). When the whole valley project was finished in 1884, Manchester had the longest chain of reservoirs in the world. The downside was that the best-quality farmland in the valley was lost and land use in the catchment area was restricted. The

The northern of the two arms of the Ladybower reservoir completes the trio that occupies the Upper Derwent Valley, providing drinking water for the inhabitants of Sheffield, Derbyshire and Nottinghamshire. Monotonous rows of conifers, planted by the Forestry Commission, line the valley.

Longdendale Valley now had a stark appearance, with coal and passenger trains billowing smoke along it and, later, rows of electricity pylons marching across the landscape. But some of the restrictions were removed after the closure of the railway line and the construction of treatment works in Arnfield and Godley in the 1960s, and the Hollingworth reservoir, which was abandoned in 1987, has since been incorporated in the Swallow Wood Nature Reserve.

Many other projects that were undertaken on a smaller scale have added to the attractions of the moorland scenery, from Marsden in the north to Tittesworth in the south. North-west of Sheffield, work that began in the late nineteenth century on a series of reservoirs at Langsett, Midhope, Underbank, Broomhead and Morehall was completed after the First World War. One of the most successful enterprises has been Stockport Corporation's scheme in the Goyt Valley, where the reservoir at Fernilee was completed in 1938 and that at Errwood in 1967. Some of the moorland reservoirs now offer recreation facilities as well as a regular supply of water that is fit to drink. They are a welcome addition to the moorland landscape.

These rocks on Kinder Scout are nicknamed The Woolpacks.

Chapter 6

Grouse Moors

The enclosure of huge acreages of commons and wastes in the late eighteenth and early nineteenth centuries under a series of private Acts of Parliament enabled great landowners to form compact moorland estates that were devoted to the shooting of grouse. The Peak District moors began to acquire their present managed appearance when grouse were first reared on an unprecedented scale in Queen Victoria's reign. The characteristic patchwork patterns of the moorland landscape are created by burning the heather in rotation on a ten- or twelve-year cycle. Controlled fires in wintertime encourage the spring growth of fresh shoots for the grouse to feed upon while patches of thick heather provide safe nesting out of sight of predators. Burning the heather was an ancient practice, for sheep too relished young shoots, but it was done on a modest scale before the introduction of shooting butts in the 1860s. The heyday of grouse-shooting was in the late-Victorian and Edwardian eras. If 'sporting estates' had not been created at that time, many moors would now be covered with conifers and others would have been encroached upon by new, rectangular pastures with meadows around their edges. Most of the prehistoric and medieval archaeological sites and the visual evidence of early forms of transport would have been lost, or at least hidden from view.

The early history of grouse-shooting

Grouse moors are unique to the British Isles and red grouse form a subspecies that is confined to these islands. They were once generally known as moor fowl or moor game. John Harrison's survey of the manor of Sheffield in 1637, for example, noted 'moore game in abundance, both blacke and red, as moorcocks, moorehenns, and young pootes [half-grown birds] upon the moores'. Black grouse were already in decline by the early nineteenth century, when John Farey observed that in Derbyshire 'Black Game, which frequent the Heathy Moors, are less frequent than formerly, and considering the very worthless nature of the herbage which they feed … the sooner they disappear altogether, the better for the community'. So far the modest attempts to re-introduce them in recent years have not been successful.

Before the second half of the seventeenth century game birds were normally caught by the use of hawks and nets. The practice of shooting them on the wing was introduced by noblemen who had learned to use flintlock guns while they were exiled on the Continent as supporters of the Royalist cause during the Civil War. The eighteenth-century antiquary, John Wilson of Broomhead Hall, claimed that an ancestor who had died in 1687 was the first local person to shoot game on the wing on the Hallamshire moors. Two hundred years later, his descendants owned the most famous grouse moor in England. Similar claims were made in the High Peak for Mr James Tunstead, a captain of dragoons in the Royalist Army and Warden of the Forest of the Peak, who in 1661 was provided with an annuity of £50 'for taking the King's game of heath poults in Derbyshire and other parts north of the Trent'. This new method of tramping across the moors with a dog and a guide, who carried the game bag and the ammunition, was slow to take hold but it grew in popularity in the late eighteenth century.

A grouse on Derwent Edge. Red grouse are a subspecies that is confined to the British Isles. An Act of 1772 established the shooting season as 12 August to 10 December. Grouse had been shot on the wing in the late seventeenth century, but with the successive improvement of guns in Victorian times the driving of game towards shooters hidden in butts became the usual practice.

As early as 1773 'wastes' in Yorkshire were rented 'for the purpose of shooting Moor Game', and in the Peak District a Baslow boundary perambulation of 1787, taken well before the parliamentary enclosure of the township's moors, recorded a point 'where the Game cabin now stands'. The success of a day's sport began to be measured by the size of the 'bag' that was recorded in game books as so many 'brace' of grouse. But in these early days the number of game birds on the moors was far lower than on the managed estates of Victorian and Edwardian times. Similar trends in the shooting of pheasants and partridges can be seen in other parts of the land.

The growing interest in shooting game on Britain's unenclosed commons and wastes inevitably led to arguments over who had a right to shoot there. The great landowners who dominated Parliament settled this question to their advantage by passing numerous Acts between 1671 and 1831. The first of these forbade the hunting of hares, pheasants, partridges and moor fowl by anyone who was not a freeholder of land valued at more than £100 per annum, or a long leaseholder of land worth more than £150 per annum. The sons and heirs of esquires and other persons 'of higher degree' were allowed to shoot game, and all lords of manors who were 'not under the degree of an esquire' were authorised to appoint gamekeepers whose duties included the seizing of guns and dogs and the searching of suspected poachers. In 1693 penalties were imposed on those who burnt heather during the breeding season between 2 February and 24 June and in 1762 the seasons in which game could be legally killed were first defined. The present dates were agreed in 1772, when it was established that the grouse-shooting season should start on 12 August and end on 10 December. Anyone caught shooting outside that season was fined heavily. What other sport, one wonders, has its season regulated by Act of Parliament?

The Game Act of 1831 took control over game away from lords of the manor and conferred it upon the owners of land. This important change in the law soon raised the rental value of moorland shooting estates to four times their previous level and led to the formation of shooting clubs. One of these was the Bradfield Game Association, whose fifteen members paid £10 per annum for their printed ticket and whose treasurer, Mr Elmhirst, a local gentleman who was descended from an old yeoman family at Hound Hill in the parish of Worsbrough, had sole charge of management and the prosecution of poachers. Elmhirst and his keeper employed forty men to protect the moor from unauthorised shooting on the opening day of the season. In the 1840s the absent owner of the neighbouring Midhope Moors let his shooting rights to a similar group of seventeen members, who were drawn from the local middle classes.

The Glorious Twelfth, the first day of the shooting season, attracted widespread interest in the towns and villages around the moors. In 1869 the Vicar of Ecclesfield and local historian, the Revd Alfred Gatty, wrote:

> On the 12th of August the moors attract crowds from Sheffield as spectators, who come by thousands, and but for the wild space over which they are distributed, they would mar the sport. But there is a good-humoured view to be taken of this motley invasion; and as all vehicles, varying from the costermonger's donkey cart to the four-horsed omnibus, are strictly kept on the roads, those who have the enjoyment of shooting need not grudge or resent, which they do not, the universal interest felt in this locality in all which concerns the sportsman's recreations.

At that time the bags were modest. Gatty thought that 'a good shoot on the 12th of August may kill forty or fifty brace of red grouse'.

Not all the moors formed part of aristocratic estates. A visitor to Kinder Scout in the summer of 1880 observed that:

> The owners of the moor are jealous to the last degree of their rights, and quarrel over the few birds which by some accident are still left as though the cause of empires were at stake. This arises from the foolish way in which the district has been parcelled out among a number of small holders, in patches not much larger than a table-cloth. One man's allotment is actually under two acres in extent, and his only chance of getting a shot is on the days when his neighbours are out shooting, and the grouse are driven over his field. Then he stands waiting for a chance … On an average during the season, there are about three guns out to each bird, and in one case a gentleman who pays £50 a year for his bit of moor only got two birds all last season.

The Kinder Enclosure Act (1840) had dealt with 1,352 acres on Kinder Moor and 87¾ acres on Kinder Bank.

John Ness Dransfield wrote that in the 1830s his uncle regularly walked 8 miles from his home to the grouse moor, shot all day with a 12-inch-bore muzzle loader weighing 12 pounds, then walked home at night. This was, he observed, somewhat different from shooting from a grouse butt all day. The new method of shooting developed with the successive improvements in gun manufacture, particularly the invention of the breech-loading shotgun. When several thousands of these new guns were in use by the early 1860s the intensive management of the moors, especially the burning of large sections of moorland on a rotation basis, began in earnest in order to provide enough birds to shoot.

Managed moors

The most radical change in the history of grouse-shooting came with the introduction of shooting butts, or 'driving holes' as Dransfield called them. These were made of stone or wood and were mostly disguised by turf up to waist level, though others were dug deep into the ground. The shooter was accompanied by a loader or two to keep up the rate of fire. Whereas in the past birds had been shot as they flew away, they were now driven by beaters towards the butts. This method was based on the *battue*, which had been introduced from France in the late eighteenth century for shooting pheasants and then for partridges. The beaters were local countrymen employed by the keepers to rouse the birds by shouting, shaking rattles and firing guns into the air. The practice whereby each sportsman had one or more loader behind him in the butt to take the discharged gun and pass him a loaded one so that he could fire continuously meant that far more birds had to be reared by the gamekeepers and driven into the line of fire. Several lines of butts were constructed to face in different directions across the moor, so that the shooters could switch from one to another as the day progressed. By the 1880s the bags shot each day were enormous.

Driving grouse towards the guns began in a modest way before butts were arranged in lines across the Peak District moors. Sir Walter Spencer-Stanhope recalled that when he started to shoot grouse at Dunford Bridge in 1836:

Three brace for a gun for a drive was considered a big bag, and I remember the first day a bag of fifty brace was got which was about 1843; it was considered a great day … As to butts, on the moors our best drives used to be by the Snailsden Road, and there was a sand-hole there for repairing the road: my father and old George Whitfield used to occupy this sand-hole, and we found that the sand-hole always

Most grouse butts are built waist high from the ground, but a group well into Moscar Moor are sunk below ground level and are supplied with drains.

had the best chances. So we thought that we would make a few more sand-holes. By about 1847 we had made a good many holes for guns in different parts of the moor, which by degrees were rearranged and the drives made more extensive.

When it became the general custom to drive grouse towards the guns to increase the size of the bag, the moors had to be managed to produce far more birds. By the mid-1860s an average of 150–170 brace were shot on a day's outing on the Spencer-Stanhope moors at Dunford Bridge. The older cocks that flew strongest towards the butts suffered heavy losses, but this allowed room for more breeding pairs in the following year. In 1873 A.J. Stuart-Wortley of Wortley Hall observed that: 'The enormous numbers of grouse to be found on the Yorkshire hills owe their existence to the fact that these moors have been consistently driven for some years past. We can state on good authority that there are moors in that county in which there are today fifty times as many birds as were found there twenty years ago.'

This new method was disliked by many as being unsporting, but when it was adopted by such leading aristocrats as the Duke of Devonshire and the

Duke of Rutland it gradually became accepted. Sir Walter Spencer–Stanhope reminisced: 'The papers used to contain references of the following kind: "We are sorry to learn that the unsportsmanlike practice of driving grouse is still continued on the Stanhope moors. This form of driving cannot be too severely reproved …". It was only when noble lords were asked to drives at Ryshworth and Edward's Moor that it suddenly became the right thing and highly popular.'

Controlled burning on a rotational basis now began in earnest. Its effectiveness as a management technique was shown when it was abandoned during the Second World War because of the lack of a labour force, and the numbers of grouse fell dramatically. Another major improvement was the digging of drains in the wettest parts of the moors, to encourage the growth of heather at the expense of cotton grass, bog-moss and purple moor grass. The drains on Ronksley Moor, for example, are contemporary with the trackways leading to the new butts. The most prominent is the Black Dyke that the Duke of Devonshire ordered to be cut across the moor for 1½ miles between two cloughs, partly following the boundary that William Senior surveyed in 1617 between the moorland commons used by Ronksley and Ridge farms. Only the eastern half of the new dike was complete when the Ordnance Survey mapped the district around 1840. Other ditches were dug to prevent the spread of fires.

On some moors special fields were created to grow black oats for the grouse. On Broomhead Moor, for instance, a 1¾-acre enclosure known locally as Sod Bank reverted to heather after the First World War but the banks are still marked on Ordnance Survey maps. Several other fields that were used for this purpose can be identified on the Duke of Rutland's Longshaw Moors Estate and the Duke of Norfolk's moors in the Upper Derwent Valley. Another innovation, which is still in use today, was the gamekeeper's trick of providing quartz grit for the birds at particular points on the moors. Grit in the gizzard helps a bird to grind the shoots of heather and, at the same time, destroys the parasitic strongyle worm that remains the greatest killer of grouse. Small upright markers on moors such as Stanage act as reminders to the keepers of the whereabouts of these heaps of grit when it comes to topping them up.

The moorland landscape was also changed by the construction of pony-and-cart tracks and the building of single-storeyed, one-roomed, stone cabins for the keepers and for shooting parties to shelter in at lunchtime. The rhododendrons that were planted near some of these cabins have spread

Abney Moor. In the late autumn or winter months sections of the grouse moors are burnt in rotation so as to encourage fresh shoots of heather for the grouse to feed upon. Controlled fires are an essential feature of moorland management, while wildfires have been a hazard over the centuries. For example, John Wilson, the antiquary of Broomhead Hall, noted: '1762 was the driest Summer ever since 1723. The moors were on fire in many places, a fire began at the Church gate at the top of Kanyer Hills and burnt all Cowell almost.'

further than intended, for example on the moors of Broomhead and Stanage. At the end of a day's sport, shooting parties could refresh themselves at one of the *Grouse Inns* that were built on the edges of the moors or, if they were with an aristocratic party, retire to the shooting lodges, such as those at Longshaw and Stanage. The Duke of Norfolk and his guests stayed regularly at Derwent Hall whilst on shooting expeditions above the Upper Derwent Valley.

In the late Victorian and Edwardian periods Broomhead Moor acquired a national reputation for its excellent management and large bags of game. The Wilson family lived at Broomhead Hall from at least 1379, when their surname was just becoming hereditary, until the death of Henry Wilson in 1819, when the estate passed to his nephew James Rimington, Esq, whose father had bought the Bolsterstone estate and whose descendants adopted the name of Rimington-Wilson. The Mr R.H. Rimington-Wilson whose initials appear on boundary stones around his moor inherited the Broomhead estate in 1877 and set about improving it. He had served seven or eight years

A derelict shooting cabin at Jarvis Clough, Moscar Moor.

in the Inniskilling Dragoons and was a keen explorer and hunter who had to have frozen toes amputated during an expedition through the Far East snows in 1880. This did not reduce his enthusiasm for shooting grouse. On 12 August 1913 nine men shot 2,843 birds on Broomhead Moor, at that time a national record for one day's shooting. The August 1904 issue of *Baily's Magazine of Sports and Pastimes* observed that 'the excellent results obtained at Broomhead are mainly due to skilled, experienced management extending over a long term of years'. Mr Rimington-Wilson and his brother took 'the keenest interest in the moors' and the knowledge of Charles Wood, the chief keeper for the last forty-five years, was 'unsurpassed'. Broomhead Moor long had the reputation of carrying more grouse per acre than any moor in Great Britain.

Stanage moors

Another family of enthusiastic 'sportsmen' were also called Wilson, but they were unrelated to their namesakes at Broomhead. Their chief income came from the Sharrow Snuff Mills, Sheffield, which their ancestor had founded in the eighteenth century and which still flourish today. In 1878 William Wilson, then of Beauchief Hall, became Master of the Barlow Hounds and built the kennels at Horsleygate in the Cordwell Valley, which are still in use. After a spinal injury from a hunting accident in 1900 had forced him to give up fox hunting, he concentrated his energies on shooting grouse. Three years earlier, he had bought the Duke of Norfolk's moorland estate covering more than 2,000 acres on Stanage, and the lodge that had been built in the middle of it in 1869. The sale was advertised as 'The Finest Sporting Estate ever offered in Sheffield or District'. Meanwhile, Wilson Mappin, the younger son of Sir Frederick Mappin, the owner of the Queen's Cutlery

In 1907 William Wilson employed the young George Broomhead to carve a group of six grouse drinking troughs in rocks near Stanedge Pole to encourage his birds to remain on his moor. Stanedge Lodge can be seen in the background.

Works and a public benefactor, had purchased the adjoining Moscar Moor. Mappin and Wilson marked their boundary at the northern end of Stanage Edge with a series of stones bearing their initials on opposite sides.

In 1907 William Wilson began an extraordinary project that has interested and often perplexed generations of ramblers. He ordered the construction of six artificial drinking troughs in a group of natural boulders near Stanedge Pole, so that his grouse would not fly away and be shot on someone else's moor. Wilson's idea seems to have come from natural basins that were formed when grit was swirled around in the wind and the rain. He is reputed to have personally chosen the rocks into which runnels were cut to channel rainwater into the troughs. An account book reveals that a teenage mason, George Broomhead, was paid 7s. 3½d. per trough to do the work. Broomhead was born in 1893 and had learned his trade with an experienced mason; carving the troughs was apprenticeship work. His first stone near Stanage Pole has two long runnels leading the rainwater down to the basin and is inscribed 'W. Wilson / 1907 / No 1'. The second trough, 40 yards to the east of the first, was fed by just one runnel, which cleverly uses the

The second trough in the first sequence has a unique design. Eventually George Broomhead carved 108 troughs on Stanage Moor for William Wilson.

natural slope of the rock. The other four troughs have simpler designs, which soon became standard ones.

Wilson must have judged this experiment a success for he soon started a much more ambitious scheme of seventy-five troughs that stretched along Stanage Edge before curving back into the moor. Five of these troughs have sunk without trace and others were found only after the thick heather was burnt. The troughs were not arranged in a systematic manner. The second stone in the sequence is 400 yards away from the first, but the unique double trough marked as number 3 is only another 15 yards further on. The stones that Wilson chose were of a variety of shapes and sizes and so the runnels and basins had to be adapted accordingly. A typical trough is about 18 inches long and 12 wide but some are much larger. The largest of all – number 19 on Stanage Edge – is 5 feet long by 2 feet wide. The troughs lie close together on the approach to High Neb but they are set far apart where the escarpment swings round to Crow Chin. Soon after 2002 some of the numbers on the stones beyond Crow Chin were obliterated in a petty act of vandalism, but the remainder can still be found in an erratic line that goes in

The first of seventy-five troughs that follow Stanage Edge before curving back into the moor stands apart from the rest, nearly a quarter-of-a-mile from the second and third.

and out of the moor and then down the slope as far as number 75, near the start of Black Clough.

The third, erratic line of twenty-seven troughs near the northern boundary of Wilson's moor is not as well-known. It starts near the Conduit at the top of Oaking Clough and zig-zags across the moor in an unpredictable manner, past the Headstone to Mare Folds by Wyming Brook. Some of the troughs are obscured by heather, bilberries, grass and even rhododendrons. George Broomhead had acquired greater skill by the time he carved the ornate letters on these stones. Numbers 13 and 14 are the most unusual of all the 108 stones on the moor, for the basins in the ground are filled by channels that descend almost vertically from an upright rock. This last sequence brings the total of troughs to 108, of which 103 were found over several years while the thick heather that disguises many of them was burnt in rotation. Wilson's idea was not taken up on any other moor in the Peak District.

Shooting only

Wilson and Mappin soon followed the practice of other landowners in ordering the removal of sheep from their moors. It was thought that as the management of heather had increased the numbers of grouse enormously, further gains would be made if the young shoots were left to the birds. It had also become obvious that overgrazing the heather by sheep was turning some of the moorland into rough grazing and sometimes into areas where even the sheep found the grass unpalatable. New fodder crops were encouraging farmers to overwinter more sheep on the moors and thus to have larger flocks there during the summer. This increase was detrimental to the quality of the moors and was unsustainable in the long term.

In the 1870s the Duke of Rutland had stopped sheep from grazing on his Longshaw moors in the summer months. Four years later the Broomhead Moor keepers claimed that the grouse were adversely affected by the 1,200 sheep and lambs from four local farms and that the dogs, running up the moor after the sheep, frightened the grouse from their nests. Back in 1797 these four farms had sheepwalks measured at 112, 156, 243 and 806 acres.

At first, Rimington-Wilson listened to the farmers' appeals but in 1879 he accepted the advice of his keepers. David Wood of Old Booth Farm was no longer able to graze 700 sheep on the moor but was reduced to keeping forty sheep on his own land. A telling point for those owners who were not themselves sportsmen was that more income could be obtained from grouse-shooting than from renting moorland for sheep or cattle grazing. A report in *Baily's Magazine* in 1904 claimed that on the best shooting moors the heather was burned solely with a view to the requirements of the grouse. The following year, a writer in *The Times* observed that 'in order to increase their grouse, the Yorkshire owners have cleared off most of the sheep'.

As the moors became more intensively managed for grouse-shooting, so the owners and their gamekeepers became more hostile to people who wished to pick bilberries or to enjoy a walk over rough moorland on their day off work. Bilberry pickers were turned away from Broomhead Moor from 1898 and from other moors not long after. The moors were now managed solely as sporting estates. Sales of game were the only source of revenue. The intensive management of the moors solely for the purpose of shooting led to the removal not only of the sheep but also of ramblers. A clash of interest soon loomed large and was not resolved until the end of the twentieth century.

Grouse were not the only game to be shot on these private moors. An account book kept by the Bowles family, the owners of Abney Moor, shows that between 1907 and 1913 the annual bags on the estate comprised 4,243 grouse, 2,331 rabbits, 263 hares, 927 pheasants, 304 partridges, nineteen black game, twelve woodcock, eleven snipe and two ducks. A farm devoted to rearing rabbits was enclosed by wire in Bretton Clough. When Thomas Gregory, Esq, of Eyam View, sold his 'country house with a sporting and agricultural estate' in 1923, the sale particulars included 'Bretton Clough Together With Grouse Moors and Plantations'. The advertisement claimed that:

> The Grouse Moors are in excellent condition as regards heather and well stocked with grouse. An average of 1,000 rabbits can be killed annually on the whole estate, besides pheasants and partridges and a few woodcock, black game and hares.

Five parts of the Duke of Rutland's Longshaw Moors estate were set aside for rabbit breeding. The largest was the 70-acre warren that stretched northwards for about a mile from the Warren Lodge that was built about 1877 below Curbar Edge. The lessee from 1914, Charles Markham, and his party once shot 400 rabbits in a day. On Boxing Day 1933 another party of four men shot 712 rabbits on the moors above the River Derwent. Meanwhile, mountain hares, whose coats turn white in winter, were imported from the

Scottish Highlands for shooting purposes on Stanage and adjoining moors. They continue to flourish on the moors above Bradfield and the Upper Derwent Valley.

By then, however, the public appetite for grouse on the table was in decline and the cost of rearing grouse was greater than the income from sales. Nevertheless, the Duke of Devonshire and some other local landowners continued to manage their moors for grouse-shooting between the two world wars. During the year ending 1 February 1935, Thomas Kingsford Wilson of Fulwood House, Sheffield, the cousin of William Wilson, kept a personal record of his bag. During those twelve months he shot 1,004 grouse and twenty-four other birds on the moors, 643 partridges, 2,112 pheasants, 146 hares, 219 rabbits, twenty woodcock and twenty-nine other birds, a total of 4,197 wildfowl. He was credited, if that is the right word, with shooting about 150,000 birds over half a century. He attributed his prowess 'to drinking Tennants' Bitter Beer when young and Wiley's Black Label Whisky later on'. His nephew continued to shoot grouse, from a chair in a specially lowered butt, after having both legs amputated because of gangrene.

The Harpur-Crewe moors

On the Staffordshire moorlands that belonged to the Harpur-Crewe family at Calke Abbey keepers' lodges were built in the early 1850s at Fawfieldhead and near Longnor. Grouse continued to be shot there after the First World War. In 1926, for example, a total of 321½ brace of grouse were shot on the moors of Flash, Gradbach and the Roaches, and in 1935 it was claimed that a considerable increase in the numbers of black game had prolonged the shooting season 'very nicely'. The previous season had been marred by: 'two fires on the home moor, both of a devastating nature. The first one burned the whole Lumm Edge drive from the Mermaid Road to Pickford's corner. The keepers, farmers, and volunteers fought with it continuously, but it was impossible to hold it. This happened on the Monday, and on the Wednesday, while they were watching the remains of fire No. 1, Revidge caught fire near the Warslow end, and beyond saving the woods, the whole of this was burned. There is not anything left of either drive.'

The correspondent added that: 'The moor is like tinder for a foot in depth, so there is practically no chance of putting out a fire if it starts.'

Grouse-shooting continued throughout the Second World War but on a much reduced scale. On 21 June 1941 Sir John Bennett of Hill Top, Butley, near Macclesfield, the leading member of the group who leased the shooting rights on the Harpur-Crewe moors, wrote to Colonel Godfrey Mosley JP TD, of Calke Abbey, advising him that cattle were being driven illegally on to the moors by Mr Ward of the Mermaid Inn and his example was likely to be followed by others, for fodder was short because of the war. Popular opinion was against the shooters and a letter in a Manchester newspaper had suggested that cattle were being sacrificed to sport on Warslow Moor.

Bennett continued: 'Unless something is done the grazing of cattle on the moors will become general, and will soon be regarded as a right. If this came about the sporting value of the moors would be practically ruined.'

His group were quite willing to give up their rights so that the estate could let the grazing at the customary price per beast, though he doubted that Ward would pay. However, the income from grazing would be only a small fraction of the loss of value to the sporting rights. As tenants they felt very strongly that during the war the farmers should have the opportunity of renting grazing on the moors if they wanted it, but whether the farmers

Mermaid Inn, Morridge, on the opposite ridge to The Roaches, takes its name from the story of a maid whose lover attempted to drown her in a nearby pool, the Blake Mere. During the Second World War, grouse-shooters were unable to prevent the landlord from grazing his cattle on the adjacent moors.

would think the grazing worth having if they could not have it for nothing remained to be seen.

The problem was not solved. During the following season, on 6 October 1942, Bennett wrote: 'I don't think we shall shoot any more this year. Our bag has been 308½ brace of Grouse, 4 Black game, 7 Hares and 2 Snipe. We have left a good stock of game for breeding. It has been a very poor season, due I think very largely to war conditions. The fact that there are cattle all over the moors means that birds are never left in peace, and this means the loss of a great many in the nesting season.' He asked whether the owners would remit the remaining half of the rent due under the lease and noted that from 25 September to 25 March 1943 all the land was required for military training, including the firing of shells from mortars and guns.

Meanwhile, a keeper reported that the illegal grazing of cattle was continuing and that 'owing to the war, he dare not feed the birds with oats, as he had always done'. The stock of birds had declined because of the severe winters of the last three years and he had seen members of the Staffordshire War Agricultural Committee on the moors testing the soil. They had already authorised the burning of The Lumbs near Mermaid Inn, 'one of the best breeding grounds for grouse on the estate'. Another problem arising from the war was revealed, without a trace of irony, by A. Bolton, Esq, of Moor Court, Oakmoor, Staffordshire, who wrote on 11 July 1943: 'I am told now that no petrol will be allowed for shooting purposes this year, but I think I shall be able to get over sometimes by taxi.'

The beaters' expenses in the 1943 season were considerably higher than in the previous year, for more men and boys were employed over eight days' shooting instead of six, and the price of beer had gone up, while an extra charge for some fox traps had been necessary, 'as the fox difficulty is still very great'. Altogether, the season's bag amounted to 245 brace, 'including grouse, pheasants, black game and partridge'. On 14 July 1944 an agreement was signed for shooting over the Warslow Moors for the coming season. The keeper, John Beswick, reported that he had killed 'a good many foxes' and that sufficient rain had fallen to keep fires at bay, but he feared that the American troops exercising 'all over the place' in May and early June had done a lot of damage to eggs and young grouse.

Nevertheless, H. Gordon Ferguson, of Cornbrook Chemical Co Ltd, Stockport, believed that 'whatever the state of the moors and the number of birds we shall, as always, enjoy ourselves thoroughly'. It turned out that they found as many birds as in the previous year. When an assessment was made on 2 October 1944 in order to claim for the loss of grouse because of military manoeuvres, it was noted that gun rents on Warslow Moor had declined from £250 in 1940 to £150 from 1942 onwards, and that the number of birds shot between 1934 and 1943 had fallen from the highest bag of 1,362 brace in 1935 to 322 brace in the last year.

In 1951 the Harpur-Crewe family had to sell 10,753 acres of farmland on their Alstonefield estate in order to pay death duties, but they kept their shooting rights on the moors until 1986, when their 4,629 acres of Staffordshire moorland passed in lieu of capital transfer tax to the Peak Park Joint Planning Board, which now manages it as the Warslow Moors Estate. The Ministry of Defence has occupied adjoining moorland since 1953 as a training area covering 2,707 acres and extending from the Leek-Buxton road in Heathylee almost to the village of Warslow.

Modern times

Since the Second World War British heather moors have been reduced by forty per cent to 700,000 acres in England and Wales and to 2½ million acres in Scotland. In the Peak District the area of heather moor fell by thirty-six per cent between 1913 and 1980 and the grouse population was reduced substantially. Today many moors are no longer managed in the old intensive manner, bags are increasingly uncertain, and the sheep have returned with a vengeance. Nevertheless, virtually all moor owners still rely on the letting of grouse-shooting to cover the costs of running their estates.

Grouse are short-lived, whether they are shot or not. Their maximum life-span is seven years and they succumb to predators and disease. Forty of the sixty black grouse that were reintroduced into the Upper Derwent Valley in 2003 soon fell victim to foxes and raptors. A few years ago, the gamekeepers on one extensive moor shot sixty foxes between October and February but felt they were still losing the battle. The main disease affecting grouse is strongylosis, caused by a gut parasite. The strongyle worm thrives in mild winters and is particularly deadly when the grouse population soars. Tick infestations in grouse chicks have also risen sharply in the last twenty years. Global warming is being blamed for the falling bird stocks, which have severely reduced the length of the shooting season, but these diseases come in irregular waves and large numbers of grouse were shot in the seasons between 2001 and 2003. The moor owners are increasingly dependent on foreign shooters, especially Italian ones, who are prepared to pay the high fees and accommodation costs.

Yet some grouse moors continue to thrive. From 2009–11 a large section of the conifer plantation of the Wentworth estate by the Strines Road near Bradfield was felled to extend the grouse moor. A report in the *Yorkshire Post* on 11 December 2009 noted that some of the year's best shooting had been on Moscar Moor, on the Yorkshire-Derbyshire boundary. After a series of disastrous seasons, the shooters had had 'a marvellous year' in which about 1,350 brace of grouse had been shot, the best bag since 1949. But even at Moscar shooting finished before the end of the season. Efforts were being made to rear a constant supply of birds after the depredations of the strongyle worm.

The moor owners argue that shooting preserves the numbers of grouse, which would otherwise succumb to strongylosis in even greater numbers and that their sport maintains the distinctive upland environment of the Peak District moors. Regular burning promotes young heather, keeps down bracken and coarse grass, and prevents the spread of silver birch. Grouse moors also provide a good habitat for many other birds, such as curlews, golden plover and wheatears. Even the RSPB agree that management for grouse-shooting is the best regime for the moorlands.

The third of a line of grouse-shooting butts high in the Upper Derwent Valley, in use during the 2011 shooting season.

Chapter 7

The Right to Roam

The first rambling clubs

The tremendous growth of the national population during Queen Victoria's reign and the rapid expansion of Manchester, Sheffield, Derby, Stoke and numerous smaller industrial towns around the Peak District affected the moors in many ways, ranging from polluted atmospheres to major engineering projects involving reservoirs, railways and quarries. Yet the working man's desire to enjoy wide open spaces on Sundays and Saturday half-holidays was thwarted when the moors were managed with a new intensity for the sole purpose of shooting grouse. Ramblers who used the new railway links to reach the moors were turned away aggressively by gamekeepers acting on the instructions of the landowners.

In the countryside immediately around the towns, as well as on the enclosed moors, some long-established footpaths came under threat from selfish individuals. The Manchester Association for the Preservation of Ancient Public Footpaths was established as early as 1826 to oppose the actions of Mr Ralph Wright, a Flixton landowner and magistrate. This body remained active for nearly forty years with monthly meetings in the old Manchester Town Hall, and in 1894 its remaining funds made a welcome contribution to the newly formed Peak District and Northern Counties Footpaths Preservation Society.

Other like-minded societies were founded up and down the country during Victoria's reign. The London and Home Counties Commons Preservation Society was formed in 1865 to launch a campaign to preserve Hampstead Heath. Three decades later it merged with the National Footpath Preservation Society to become the Commons, Open Spaces and Footpaths Preservation Society (now The Open Spaces Society). Prominent members included Sir Robert Hunter, Octavia Hill and Canon Rawnsley, the three founders of The National Trust in 1895. The society campaigned for access to common land throughout the whole of Britain. Meanwhile, London ramblers were forming groups such as The Sunday Tramps (1879), a socially exclusive, male-dominated society consisting largely of writers, philosophers, academics and professional men in the law and politics, and the Forest Ramblers Club (1884), an Epping Forest organisation whose members were drawn from the retail trade and who met on the mid-week early closing day. Other professional and businessmen groups included the Yorkshire Ramblers Club (1892) and the Manchester Rucksack (1902).

The outdoors movement began to attract a wide range of people. The Liverpool YMCA Rambling Club (1874), the Manchester YMCA Rambling Club (1880), the Co-operative Holidays Association

A characteristic footpath sign erected on the slopes of Kinder Scout by the Peak District and Northern Counties Footpaths Preservation Society.

(1893) and the Midland Institute of Ramblers (1894) flourished. In 1905 representatives from about a dozen English groups formed the Federation of Rambling Clubs, whose chief objectives were to maintain and preserve ramblers' rights and privileges, and to obtain cheap, concessionary rail fares.

Meanwhile, rock climbing had become a popular sport. In the 1880s and 1890s Wharncliffe Crags was the most sought-after climbing venue in the country, but it soon lost out to Stanage and other Peak District escarpments. The first, though unsuccessful, steps towards a concerted access movement began in 1884 when James Bryce, Liberal MP for Tower Hamlets and Regius Professor of Civil Law at Oxford, introduced the Access to Mountains (Scotland) Bill in Parliament. In a renewed attempt in 1892 Bryce denied that 'there exists or is recognised by our law or in natural justice, such a thing as an unlimited power of exclusion'. But such bills were always defeated by the landowners who dominated Parliament.

In the middle years of Victoria's reign, long before working-class rambling groups were formed, middle-class people could usually walk across the Peak District moors without too much trouble, especially if they tipped the gamekeepers. In 1880 Louis J. Jennings wrote in his *Rambles Among the Hills in the Peak of Derbyshire and the South Downs*: 'The Bradfield and Derwent Moors lie away to the north, Abney Moor to the south, and the Hallam Moors to the east, all with good paths over them in various directions.' These paths had not yet been closed by the landowners. But when he walked up Kinder Scout from the Snake Inn he found that his path was:

> soon lost amid the heather and furze, and the traveller must make out a track for himself as well he can ... My next visit to the 'Scout' was made in the early summer from Hayfield ... The first discovery which my inquiries brought to light was that the Kinder Scout is regarded as strictly private property, and that it is divided up among numerous holders, almost all of whom are at loggerheads with each other and with the public ... There are said to be certain public rights of foot-way, but they do not appear to lead to the best points, and even in regard to these are constant disputes. Moreover, they are hard to find amidst a labyrinth of heath and ferns. It is not unusual for the gamekeepers to turn strangers back even when they are upon the paths which are supposed to be fairly open to all ... You get permission from three or four different holders, and find that there is still another who bars the way ... personally I experienced no inconvenience whatever.

The Peak District and Northern Counties Footpaths Preservation Society

Disputes over rights of way increased when the grouse-shooting moors were managed more carefully in the late-Victorian era. In 1877 the ancient path from Hayfield to the Snake Inn via William Clough around the northern side of Kinder Scout was closed by landowners in an illegal action that was nevertheless approved by the Derbyshire quarter sessions three years later. On 29 July 1894 an anonymous letter in the *Manchester Guardian* pointed out that access to Kinder was part of a larger problem. More and more stretches of moorland were being closed to ramblers and no organisation existed to preserve old-established rights of way. Five days later W.H. Chadwick of Gorton convened a meeting in the Piccadilly Restaurant, Manchester, 'to consider the best means of securing the public rights of way over Kinder Scout from Hayfield to the Snake Inn'. It was resolved 'that a society be formed to preserve public rights of way within 50 miles of Manchester and such society be called The Manchester and District Footpaths Preservation

Society'. The name was soon changed to The Peak District and Northern Counties Footpaths Preservation Society, a body that flourishes to this day and whose characteristic green signposts can be seen on the local moors. Members of the new society met with the Duke of Devonshire and asserted the right of walkers to the William Clough passage over his moors. They offered to prove this at law but sought a compromise that would satisfy the sporting interest, for they recognised that grouse-shooting was the only value of properties on the bleak plateau of Kinder Scout.

On 24 September 1896 the *Manchester Guardian* reported that the society had:

> happily succeeded in its first enterprise. The favourite route over Kinder Scout, from Hayfield to the Snake Inn, has been secured for ever to the public. All that remains to be done is to form a path, erect signposts, and build a small bridge over the Lady Brook near the Snake Inn. Everyone will then be able to take this delightful walk through some of the finest and wildest scenery in the Peak District without let or hindrance. This peaceful victory over the landowners, who threatened for a time to close the path, although within the memory of man the public had always enjoyed the right of way, speaks volumes for the energy and tact displayed by the officials of the Society. The appeal the Society now makes for £500 to pay the legal and other costs incurred in securing the footpath, will gain a ready response.

The path was formally re-opened on 29 May 1897 by the president, Sir William H. Bailey, the Salford engineer who lived at Sale Hall (Cheshire), and the occasion was attended by a large body of subscribers and friends.

An article in the *Journal of Manchester Geographical Society* commented on a field trip later that year:

> To those of us who are getting old it seems so strange that so stiff a fight should have been necessary for this footpath right, because thirty or forty years ago the Scout was a happy hunting-ground for those who were then young. From Glossop to the Snake to the Kinder Downfall, from Hayfield to the Snake we wandered at our own sweet will; we were never troubled about footpaths and we were never challenged, but time works wonders and the report of the meeting of the Association is, from this point of view, curious reading, yet it shows how this footpath (like

The moorland footpath along William Clough on the north-western side of Kinder Scout, which was re-opened in 1897 after a prolonged campaign by the PD & NCFPS.

the Roman road over Blackstone Edge) had been nearly lost for the want of someone to look after it.

The PD&NCFPS soon discovered that the newly formed reservoir companies were as hostile to ramblers on their water-gathering grounds as were the grouse moor owners. For instance, when the reservoirs in the Upper Derwent Valley were constructed, protracted negotiations were necessary before all the threatened paths were secured or satisfactory substitutes were created. Ramblers were turned back on the eastern side of the reservoirs from Slippery Stones until the society took up the matter with the owner and enforced the right of way.

G.H.B. Ward and the Sheffield Clarion Ramblers

In 1900 George Herbert Bridges Ward formed what he described as 'the first Sunday workers' rambling club in the North of England', the Sheffield

Clarion Ramblers. It was to become the most active group in the access movement during the first half of the twentieth century and Ward became widely known as The King of the Ramblers, the most vociferous champion of the right to roam. His group took their name from the socialist weekday paper *The Clarion*, which Robert Blatchford, a Manchester journalist, had founded four years earlier. Its socialism was of the William Morris rather than the Karl Marx variety and it was popular with members of the outdoors movement. Numerous Clarion Cycling Clubs, Clarion Glee Clubs and Clarion Cafés were set up in various parts of the country. In 1919 the Manchester Clarion Café (opened eleven years earlier) was where the Manchester Ramblers' Federation was formed. Bert Ward inserted an advertisement in the *Clarion* inviting readers to join him on a strenuous 20-mile ramble around Kinder Scout on Sunday 2 September 1900, meeting at Sheffield Midland station to catch the 8.30 am train to Edale. Eleven men and three women took up the invitation. They probably already knew each other.

The choice of travel by rail was significant, for the line through the Hope Valley to Manchester (with a station at Edale) had been opened just a few years before. Now, ordinary people from the industrial cities had quick and cheap access into the heart of the Peak District, including Kinder Scout. The first ramble (a hard walk that Ward had reconnoitred the week before) followed an ancient footpath along the southern side of Kinder Scout, past Barber Booth and Upper Booth farms, up Jacob's Ladder to Edale Cross, and down the other side of the Pennines to lunch and a sing-song at Hayfield. The party returned via the William Clough footpath around the northern side of Kinder Scout to the Snake Inn, the path that had been re-opened three years earlier. Tea for fourteen was ordered at the inn, to the surprise of the staff who had to bake fresh bread and cakes, and after another sing-song and long walk the return train was caught at Hope, arriving back in Sheffield at 8 pm. What a day! Ward kept repeating 'Pioneers, oh pioneers'. He was asked to organise five more walks the following year. From such modest beginnings a mass movement was created.

Bert Ward was born in 1876 in Sheffield, where his ancestors had long been employed in the local metal trades. His grandfather had a small business making fenders and his father was a skilled craftsman and supervisor. Bert's childhood was spent at Glen Cottage, Park Farm, near the present Park Hill flats, surrounded by fields above the smoky, industrial city. He had a working-class background but his family were a little better-off than most

The opening of the Sheffield to Manchester railway through the Hope Valley in 1894 provided working-class ramblers with cheap and quick access to Edale, though Kinder Scout (seen on the skyline) was forbidden territory. The Sheffield Clarion Ramblers came this way on their first outing in 1900.

of their neighbours and they lived away from the crowded terraced houses that clustered around the steelworks. At the time of the 1901 census his parents had died and he was living in the family home with his younger sister and a housekeeper. His occupation was given as 'fitter and turner in an iron works'. His sister was a school teacher.

Soon after the taking of the census, Bert Ward married the daughter of a Dronfield stone mason, Fanny Bertha Platts, with whom he had four daughters and two sons. In 1915 they moved out of smoky Sheffield to Storth Lodge, Moorwood, on the edge of the moors in the parish of Holmesfield, where they spent the rest of their lives. The couple were well-suited for they both enjoyed singing and playing the piano and attending musical concerts and opera, and they often walked together on holidays in Wales, the Lake District and the Yorkshire Dales.

Bert's father, who was also named George Bridges Ward, was a lasting influence who introduced the boy to the joys of writing poetry and rambling. Bert also followed his father in becoming a Sunday School teacher, but in his twenties he turned from religion to politics and became attached to the growing socialist movement as an active trade unionist with the Amalgamated Society of Engineers. From 1903 to 1911 he served as the secretary of the newly formed Sheffield branch of the Labour Representation Committee, the forerunner of the Labour Party. Later he became distrustful of politicians but kept his moderate, non-violent socialist beliefs all his life. These beliefs were reinforced by those of another socialist who had settled in Holmesfield – Edward Carpenter, the radical thinker of Millthorpe.

An unusual aspect of Bert Ward's early life was his trip as a young man to the Canary Islands, an excursion that was not normally made in those days. It seems to have been paid for by small legacies from his father and maternal grandfather. This stimulated a great interest in Spain and particularly in Spanish politics. He became fluent in Spanish, befriended two Spanish politicians, and in 1911 published a book entitled *The Truth About Spain*. The considerable collection of books that came to light when his daughter died at Moorwood a few years ago shows that he was a well-read man with wide interests.

The year that his book was published he changed career in an unexpected direction. He became a civil servant at the Sheffield and Brightside Labour Exchange. Then, during the First World War, he was posted to the Ministry of Munitions in Whitehall. Upon his return in 1919 he became a conciliation officer in industrial disputes. This seems a far cry from his days as an active socialist and, indeed, it brought scorn from many who had known him when he was young, but he seems to have been effective at the job. So we have a curious picture of a man who spent his working life trying to reach peaceful agreements, who accepted his wife's control of domestic arrangements, but who then strode purposefully through his front gate out onto the moors in search of an aggressive argument with a gamekeeper. It was well-known amongst ramblers that Bert Ward could be 'a cantankerous old so-and-so'.

Rambling was not just a leisure pursuit for Bert Ward. To him, looking and thinking as he walked were as important as the physical exercise. He spoke of 'the trinity of legs, eyes and mind'. Vigorous walking across the moors, battling with the elements, was manly and character-building. His slogan 'a rambler made is a man improved' appeared on the front of the Sheffield Clarion Ramblers' publications from 1906 onwards. Another favourite was 'The man who never was lost never went very far'. Exceptionally long, arduous walks were organised under the slogan 'to be a Clarion Rambler, and learn to be a man'. Ward issued an annual prospectus for the group

Jacob's Ladder. Bert Ward led the Sheffield Clarion Ramblers along this ancient public footpath from Edale to Hayfield on their historic walk around Kinder Scout in 1900.The steep path above the bridge acquired its biblical name because the first steps in the hillside were constructed by Jacob Marshall, a local farmer and pedlar.At the summit, a traditional cairn guides ramblers in bad weather.

in 1902 and by 1912 these had grown into what are now a famous series of handbooks, each of which contained about 100 pages of notes, essays on the history and natural history of the local landscape, local lore, poems, stories and anecdotes, maps and photographs, advertisements and articles about walking in other parts of Britain. Ward believed that the leaders of every ramble should have interesting information to pass on about the local and natural history of the countryside. Some old ramblers said that he always seemed to choose the coldest place on a ramble to give them a detailed lecture.

Ward's Sunday School teaching had ended in 1897 when his fire-and-brimstone vicar turned him out. Ward said later, tongue in cheek, that the church had played an active role in helping to establish the first working-class Sunday rambling club in his area. It has been said that Ward preached the gospel of rambling and produced 'commandments', the tone of which seemed to be remarkably akin to the stern character-building advice preached in the church he had left. For example:

The leader will take the ramble as printed – wet or fine. He has charge of the arrangements and will make provision for tea, etc., but cannot be responsible for a large party. He should provide a reading or give useful information (place-names, etc.) from the SCR booklets or other sources. New members should not defile moor or field with paper or orange peel or leave gates open.

Ward was a fiery orator and a determined advocate of the right to roam but he insisted that responsibility for the care of the countryside went with this privilege. When he lived at Park Farm, Sheffield, he wrote a letter to the local paper complaining of vandalism by people using two public footpaths and urging action to prevent thoughtless behaviour. His old hatred of litter surfaced in 1927 in his comment on the opening up of the Burbage Valley near Longshaw: 'We hope that the 'bus holiday' crowds will not be allowed to become so thick, or so foolish, as to require the paid services of a wheelbarrow trundler of waste paper.' And at a committee meeting in 1923: 'a discussion arose upon the post war young members of the Club and their lack of thought in singing comic songs, footballing and light hearted conduct, which, misunderstood by the country man, was apt to give a wrong impression of the Club. It was agreed that members should take action individually, for the present.'

Bert spent many hours in the archives section of Sheffield Central Library searching for historical evidence in whatever documents and maps were available. He looked, for instance, at the Holmesfield Enclosure Award of 1820 and Holmesfield's manor court rolls, stretching back into the Middle Ages. The information that he gleaned from such records provided him with valuable ammunition in his campaign to get moorland paths re-opened. He was a pioneer in finding this vital type of evidence in the battle to keep footpaths open and in 1912 he founded the Hallamshire Footpath Preservation Society to further this sort of work. His involvement in ascertaining rights of way broadened into a wider interest in the historical landscape. He published an article, for instance, in the *Transactions of the Hunter Archaeological Society* on Mortimer's Road, the ancient bridleway over the Strines to Penistone that was made a turnpike road in the 1770s. He was an active member of this Sheffield-based archaeological and local history society and he was a prominent founder member of what was to become the Sheffield and Peak District Branch of the Council for the Preservation of Rural England.

The Sheffield Clarion Ramblers were always to the fore in the long campaign for access to mountain and moorland. They held their first trespass, which Ward organised in 1907, with an overnight ramble over Bleaklow, the forbidding moor at the summit of the Snake Pass, just north of Kinder Scout. Ward walked where he wanted and was strong enough and sufficiently fierce-looking to deter assault by all but the most hostile gamekeeper. But although he was loud in argument, he did not advocate violence. Instead he urged his fellow ramblers to adopt a superior attitude with aggressive gamekeepers, which was easier said than done. He sought the moral high ground, convinced that the landowners were acting illegally in blocking ancient paths and bridleways across the moors. He was undaunted by the rank of the landowner, on one occasion accepting an invitation to put his case to the Duke of Norfolk in Derwent Hall. He was always one of the speakers – and usually the most forceful – at the rallies held in Winnats Pass from 1926 every year until the outbreak of war in 1939, which were jointly organised by the Manchester and Sheffield Ramblers' Federations in support of Trevelyan's Access Bill in Parliament.

His favoured course was to negotiate limited access agreements with landowners, such as that over the Dore to Hathersage bridleway, which was agreed in 1928. Where there was no evidence of a former right of way he was prepared to accept a permit allowing him to cross a moor, as a first step in the wider campaign for the right to roam over uncultivated land. Now that cheap travel by rail into the heart of the Peak District had made the forbidden lands accessible to ramblers, they demanded not just the restoration of old rights of way but the freedom to wander at will over some of the wildest terrain in England.

In the 1920s trespassing on the forbidden summits of the moors was far more common than is now generally recognised, though rambling clubs were wary of doing this as organised groups for fear of legal action. The minutes of the Sheffield Clarion Ramblers for 1921, for example, record (ungrammatically) that it was 'Agreed that there be two Midnight Rambles, despite some fears that the Kinder and Bleaklow tops, thanks to the Club's years of propaganda and practical education were now constantly trodden by Sheffield and Manchester ramblers, that since the end of the war the gamekeepers were keeping strict watch and public opinion, if steadily growing, was not sufficiently pronounced for an officially organised club party to go with importunity and defy the consequences'.

The most persistent enforcer of injunctions against trespassers was James Watts of Cheadle, a Manchester businessman who owned the part of Kinder Scout that included the Downfall. His concern was that uncontrolled access would mean that the moor would 'soon lose its entire sporting value', a fear that has not been realised on grouse-shooting moors since the right to roam was established in 2000. Watts was a fierce protagonist who in 1923 compelled Bert Ward to sign an injunction not to trespass there or to incite others to do so. The Sheffield Clarion Ramblers formally placed on record its 'detestation at the selfishness, arrogance and lack of public spirit shown by Mr Watts and expressed their

G. H. B. Ward (centre, with white shirt) and fellow members of the Sheffield Clarion Ramblers pose in a peat grough on Kinder Scout during a trespass on 13 January 1924. The photograph belongs to the family of Willis Marshall (second right) and is copyright of Ann Beedham, *Days of Sunshine and Rain: Rambling in the 1920s* (2011).

deepest sympathy to Ward, accepting that no other course was open to him but to sign the undertaking'. A fund was opened to defray his legal expenses and a subsequent meeting 'voiced its indignation at the arrogant manner in which a landowner in the year 1923, by means of obscure Acts of Parliament, had contrived to secure a legal victory at the expense of our public-spirited Hon. Secretary and a Fellow of the Royal Geographical Society at that'. Despite the injunction, Ward was photographed with a group of young Sheffield Clarion Ramblers in a peat grough on Kinder Scout a few months later on 13 January 1924. In the *Sheffield Clarion Ramblers' Handbook* for 1928–9 Ward observed that there was 'no secret concerning the fact that ramblers do traverse Kinder Scout now ... The late Mr James Watts prohibited access to the plateau summit, threatened injunctions against ramblers, and inserted advertisements with photos of ramblers in the Manchester newspapers and offered a reward of £5 for the names and addresses of trespassers'.

Four years later, just before the mass trespass from Manchester, Ward noted that Watts' reward was that the 'alluring peat-trenched summit of Kinder Scout' was 'overrun with ramblers of all types'. In the same handbook he reported 'Another search on Kinder Scout' on Sunday 22 November 1931, when a variously estimated group of 600 to 1,000 ramblers under the leadership of the Manchester Ramblers' Federation looked for a missing 17-year-old youth. Guided by the sectional leaders, who clearly knew the summit well, they made a 'thorough search of the top and sides of the plateau'. Even if the estimates were too high, it is likely that the number of ramblers involved in the search was greater than that of the mass trespass in the following year.

The historian A.J.P. Taylor and some colleagues at Manchester University were amongst the regular trespassers. In his autobiography Taylor recalled: 'We managed at least one all-day walk each weekend, trespassing on Kinder Scout or Bleaklow. I remember one such walk when Ray Eastwood (professor of law) made us creep along under a wall for half a mile on the alarm that gamekeepers were on the watch for us. It turned out that there were no gamekeepers and that Ray was playing a prank on Bullock, the professor of Italian, also with us, who was extremely law abiding.'

The Sheffield Clarion Ramblers were long involved in a struggle over the moorland route from the Snake Pass to Glossop, known since at least the seventeenth century as Doctor's Gate, which had been closed illegally by Lord Howard. In 1909 they walked the full length of the path, then the Manchester Rambling Club (which had been founded in 1907) did the same for the next five years. In 1911 Lord Howard agreed to re-open and repair the route, but he refused access during the breeding and shooting seasons. The campaign was renewed after the First World War and in 1921 Ward led a joint walk of Sheffield and Manchester ramblers along the route and gave the address. The protracted battle over this ancient right of way ended in victory for the ramblers in 1927. In the same year the Duke of Rutland, who had long been actively hostile to ramblers, had to sell his 11,533-acre moorland estate to pay for death duties, and a 'Longshaw Committee' was immediately formed to raise funds to purchase the park and to hand it over to The National Trust so that ramblers would be free to walk over it.

In these early disputes the rambling organisations were well-served by officers who were lawyers and who knew how costly legal action would be. It was not until 1929 that the Peak District and Northern Counties Footpaths Preservation Society resorted to a court case. This involved a footpath

Doctor's Gate. Before the Snake Pass turnpike road was opened in 1821, this was the stony route from Sheffield to Glossop that crossed the summit of the Pennines between Kinder Scout and Bleaklow. There is no proof that this was the Roman road between *Navio* (Brough) and *Melandra Castle* (Glossop). It was known in 1627 as Doctor Talbot's Gate. The re-opening of this ancient route was an early triumph for Sheffield and Manchester ramblers.

dispute at Benfield, where the local council refused to take any action to establish the public right of way. Several demonstrations were arranged over a five-year period, including one that involved more than 200 people, but the obstructions were always replaced by the farmer until a member took out a summons against him and won the case in court.

In the later 1920s and 1930s cheap rail and bus fares encouraged many more working-class people to walk for pleasure in the British countryside. Rambling became a mass activity, encouraged by such bodies as the Holiday Fellowship, the Co-operative Holidays' Association and the Youth Hostel Association. It has been estimated that about 10,000 people visited the Peak District each summer weekend. Federations of rambling clubs were formed in several provincial cities, led by Manchester (1919), Liverpool (1922) and Sheffield (1926, a union of fifteen clubs Ward was instrumental in creating). In 1927 representatives from many parts of the country met at Hope in a historic first meeting, chaired by the president of the PD&NCFPS.

It was becoming apparent that the outdoor movement needed a national body to represent the interests of ramblers. This came about in September 1931 when delegates from around the country attended a meeting at Longshaw Lodge, as a result of which the National Council of Ramblers' Federations (the forerunner of the Ramblers' Association) was established. This meeting was convened by Bert Ward and Stephen Morton, a Sheffield Clarion Rambler and the Secretary of the Sheffield Ramblers' Federation. Together with Tom Stephenson, a Lancashire man who had been imprisoned as a conscientious objector in the First World War and who was now a part-time agent for the Labour Party, and Phil Barnes, a young draughtsman whom Stephenson described as 'a dedicated Sheffield rambler and persistent trespasser', these working men were the chief campaigners for access to the forbidden moors. Yet, the legend of the mass trespass of 1932 has it that the early rambling clubs consisted of middle-aged, middle-class, easily cowed people who achieved nothing. Such a view can only be put down to ignorance of what had gone on before.

Kinder Scout and the legend of the mass trespass

The man who organised the mass trespass was a likeable, stocky fellow, well-under 5 feet tall, called Benny Rothman. He was born on 1 June 1911, the middle of five children of Jewish Romanian parents who had come to Britain via America at the turn of the century. His father ran hardware stalls at Glossop and Shaw markets. Benny won a scholarship to the Central High School for Boys in Manchester, but had to leave at the age of 14 to earn his living as an errand boy at a city garage. He soon saved enough money to buy a bike and cycle to north Wales, where he climbed Snowdon.

'I was the only person up there,' he said. 'It just hit me, that great open view with the sea all around.'

As a teenager he joined the Young Communist League and was once arrested and fined a week's wages for chalking a slogan on the pavement outside a police station. He was a regular attender at the Sunday night debates at the Manchester Clarion Café, where Independent Labour Party members, Trotskyists, socialists and communists of all kinds harangued each other.

As the secretary of the British Workers' Sports Federation, a subsidiary of the Young Communist League, Rothman organised a camp for the London section at Rowarth in the High Peak over Easter 1932, where he attempted to lead a small group up on to Bleaklow but was turned away by abusive and threatening gamekeepers. This was the spark that ignited the mass trespass a few weeks later.

'Back at the camp,' Rothman recalled, 'we decided that if, instead of six or seven, there'd been forty or fifty of us, they wouldn't have been able to do it.'

The mass trespass, and the reactions to it, can only be understood in the political context of the times. The British Workers' Sports Federation had no previous interest in the access movement and after 1932 it played little, if any, part in the subsequent campaign. It had been formed as a result of a split within an earlier organisation, which had been established in 1923 under the auspices of the Clarion Cyclists. Its stated goal was international unity and peace through sport, but the organisation was infiltrated by the Communist Party, whose members advocated a more militant approach. In 1930 Labour Party members and trade unionists left the organisation and regrouped. The BWSF remained communist.

The various ramblers' federations feared a take-over by Communists – and indeed by Fascists who were also trying to infiltrate the outdoor movement – and they believed that their recent gains, such as at Doctor's Gate and Longshaw, would be imperilled by militant action. By his own admission, Benny Rothman knew nothing about the history of the access movement and he acknowledged later that it had been a mistake to antagonise the main body of ramblers, who should have been useful allies rather than opponents. In his own words, 'We were newcomers to rambling.'

In mid-April the 20-year old Rothman went to the offices of

A plaque commemorates the place where Benny Rothman stood on a ledge in a quarry to inspire the mass trespassers with a speech before they moved on to Sandy Heys.

the *Manchester Evening News* where he was interviewed about his proposal for 'direct action', beginning with a demonstration at Hayfield recreational ground at 2 pm on Sunday 24 April. The Manchester and District Ramblers' Federation condemned it and Bert Ward and the Sheffield Clarion Ramblers refused their support. Rothman duplicated leaflets to hand out at railway stations. One given out at Eccles read: 'If you've not been rambling before, start now, you don't know what you've missed. Come with us for the best day out that you have ever had.'

The trespass was to be a political statement, a merry jaunt, not a strenuous hike lasting all day. Seasoned ramblers must have sniffed at the idea of a two o'clock start and a return before nightfall, covering a mere 6 miles.

It is difficult for a historian to make sense of the varied accounts, both at the time and later, of what took place on the day and at the subsequent trial, for even the recorded dates of the court cases and the names of those involved are sometimes contradictory.

The mass trespass attracted support from fifteen Lancashire clubs and two from Sheffield. Estimates of the numbers involved vary considerably, as they always do on public occasions. Benny Rothman claimed that 600–800 followed his lead, but the *Manchester Guardian* guessed 400–500. Other claims were lower. The police were out in force at Manchester London Road and other railway stations, where they intended to serve an injunction on Rothman, but he went on his bicycle. The Hayfield Parish Council at its meeting on the previous Tuesday had taken steps to stop the protest meeting on its recreation ground, in accordance with its by-laws. The Deputy Chief Constable of Derbyshire, the clerk of the Parish Council, and a large body of policemen were there to enforce the law.

The protesters therefore abandoned the speeches and set off in fine weather in the direction of Kinder Scout, singing as they marched. One press report claimed that they sang 'The Red Flag', but Benny Rothman remembered several renditions of 'It's a long way to Tipperary'. A future distinguished musical composer, Sir Michael Tippett, was amongst those who took part. The protesters were overwhelmingly young men. A few young women were kept to the rear in case violence broke out.

It was only when they arrived at Hayfield that the leaders decided which route to take. They were warned off trespassing on the water-gathering grounds of Stockport Corporation's reservoir below Kinder, which had been opened in 1911, and decided not to complicate matters by protesting against this institution as well. They proceeded along the lane to a quarry, where Benny Rothman was lifted on to a protruding rock to give an inspiring speech. Then off they went along the footpath to William Clough, oblivious of the history of the earlier struggle to keep this way open.

Having passed the reservoir, they turned off the path and began the ascent of Sandy Heys on the western edge of the Kinder plateau. At the top of the first steep part forty or fifty of the trespassers were confronted by eight gamekeepers armed with sticks. One of the trespassers recorded: 'The keepers had sticks, while the ramblers fought mainly with their hands, though two keepers were disarmed and their sticks turned against them. Other ramblers took belts off and used them, while one spectator at least was hit by a stone. There will be plenty of bruises carefully nursed in Gorton and other parts of Manchester to-night, but no-one was at all seriously hurt except one keeper, Mr E[dward] Beaver, who was knocked unconscious and damaged his ankle. He was helped back to the road and taken by car to Hayfield and to Stockport Infirmary. He was able to return home to-night after receiving treatment. After the fight the police chiefs, who had accompanied the mass trespassers, left them alone to their great though premature relief. The fight over, we continued up-hill, passing on the way a police inspector bringing down one rambler, who was subsequently detained at Hayfield Police Station.'

Another trespasser recalled: 'The keepers offered little or no resistance and we just walked past them.'

The trespassers followed the public footpath past Kinder Reservoir before ascending Sandy Heys (left). Kinder Downfall is seen in the distance (right).

Benny Rothman, who had not been involved in the short fight, claimed: 'We were then on the top of Kinder Scout.' In fact they had only reached the north-western tip of the plateau. It seems that, unlike the numerous ramblers who had trespassed on Kinder Scout before them, they had little idea of where they were. They needed to turn right towards Kinder Downfall, the most famous place on the escarpment, and to proceed on to the moor itself. Instead they turned left and quickly descended to Ashop Head, where they held a jubilant victory meeting. It is ironic that this took place on the public footpath that had been re-opened in 1897.

Tom Stephenson claimed that the Manchester trespassers never got on to Kinder Scout. He was right.

At Ashop Head the Manchester trespassers were joined by a party of about thirty from Sheffield, who had walked up the public footpath known as Jacob's Ladder from Edale and who must have been bewildered when the main party moved off in the opposite direction. Having been congratulated by Rothman, the trespassers were warned that some of them might be unfortunate enough to be fined, and to meet any costs the hat was passed round. The group then returned along the public footpath to Hayfield, where a policeman suggested they follow his car in procession, still 200-strong and singing triumphantly until five men, identified by a keeper, were arrested; as we have seen, another man had been detained earlier. One of the trespassers wrote later: 'The rest of the now doleful procession was carefully shepherded through Hayfield while, as the church bells rang for Evensong, the jubilant villagers crowded every door and window to watch the police triumph.'

This was not a matter of social class, as has sometimes been suggested, for Hayfield was an industrial village consisting largely of workers' cottages. Rather, it was the ancient antagonism between town and country. The villagers were delighted that the rowdy Manchester youths had got their 'come-uppance'. Those arrested were aged between 19 and 23: John Anderson (21), Jud Clynes (23), Tony Gillett (19), Harry Mendel (23), David Nassbaum (19) and Benny Rothman (20). On 11 May they were brought before a court at New Mills on a charge of riotous assembly and were sent to await trial at Derby assizes. There the jury consisted of military officers and country gentlemen who had nothing in common with the young Manchester communists, half of whom were Jewish (as the judge pointed out). The jury had no hesitation in finding five of the defendants guilty of riotous behaviour, but the other was released on lack of evidence. John Anderson was sentenced to six months imprisonment for occasioning bodily harm on the keeper, Benny Rothman was put in Leicester gaol for four months, and the other three received shorter sentences. One of the six, Tony Gillett, was a university student who came from a wealthy banking family. He was offered the chance to apologise but he refused and so was sent to prison.

Before the trial the trespassers had not received much public support. The mainstream rambling bodies, which had used organised trespass before in defence of footpaths, were angry that these young Manchester communists had, as they saw it, ruined their lobbying work. Philip Daley of the Manchester Ramblers' Federation (and later a member of the Ramblers' Association Executive) spoke for many when he said that it was 'a positive hindrance and deterrent to the discussions and negotiations to secure the freedom of the hills'. The turning point came with widespread disgust at the harsh sentences, which were out of all proportion to the crimes. The *Manchester Guardian* captured the public mood when it said that the trespass had resembled a university rag and should have been treated as such. By trying to teach these Manchester youths a lesson, the military men and country gentlemen on the jury had shot themselves in the foot. The sentences received national publicity, nearly all of it hostile. A stunt that would soon have been forgotten became entrenched in public memory.

At a gathering for the seventieth anniversary of the mass trespass in 2002, the eleventh Duke of Devonshire said that the decision to prosecute 'was a great shaming on my family and the sentences handed out were harsh'.

While awaiting the trial at Derby, the BWSF sent members to the annual Winnats Access Rally on the last Sunday in June, where they heckled the speakers, Professor C.E.M. Joad and P.M. Oliver MP. Nevertheless, the Manchester Ramblers' Federation made an appeal for clemency to the Home Secretary, which fell on deaf ears. Stephen Morton thought that the mass trespass was 'entirely political' and had achieved nothing. Tom Stephenson was dismissive of the whole affair. 'The mass trespass,' he wrote, 'was dramatic, yet it contributed little, if anything, to the access campaign.' He claimed that public interest soon faded and that perhaps the best thing to stem from the episode was Ewan MacColl's song 'The Manchester Rambler', whose stirring chorus went:

I'm a rambler, I'm a rambler from Manchester way,
I get all my pleasure the hard, moorland way,
I may be a wage slave on Monday,
But I'm a free man on Sunday.

At the time of the trespass MacColl was 17-year-old Jimmie Miller from Salford. Unlike many of the others he had been on previous moorland rambles and he was involved with the publicity before the event. He went on to become a well-known actor, singer and writer of protest songs, such as 'The ballad of Ho Chi Minh' and 'The ballad of Stalin', but he did not take an active part in the continuing campaign for access.

Far from being the start of a mass movement for access to the moors, the demonstration from Manchester was not repeated. When he was released from gaol, Benny Rothman had no job to return to so he became a full-time political activist for the Young Communist League, further north in Burnley. There he helped to organise a prolonged but unsuccessful strike of textile workers at Moor Loom before returning to Manchester, where he worked as a garage mechanic, then in an aircraft factory and at Metropolitan Vickers in Trafford Park. He was much involved in anti-Fascist demonstrations and trade union activities but was no longer involved in organised trespassing. The Manchester youths who had taken part in the mass trespass were not called upon to repeat their experience.

In 1931 Bert Ward and fellow members of the Sheffield Clarion Ramblers began to erect and rebuild several cairns on the Duke of Norfolk's road from Bar Dyke to Abbey Clough. They did this to assert a right of way that had been closed illegally, to show the track at tricky points and to prevent ramblers from straying into Hobson Moss Dyke at the head of Agden Clough, 'where, in nesting time, the grouse are most numerous'. Since its re-opening in 1957 this track has become well-defined.

The initiative passed back to the older rambling organisations that were grouped together within the Sheffield and (to a lesser extent) the Manchester Ramblers' Federations, though the Sheffield Clarion Ramblers remained aloof. A second mass trespass, this time across the Bradfield Moors, was organised for 18 September. This route had long been championed by Bert Ward, who had undertaken much historical research to show that this public way from the Upper Derwent Valley to Bar Dyke had been laid out in the Bradfield Enclosure Award of 1826 and had since been closed illegally. Ward chaired the meeting of the Sheffield Ramblers' Federation that discussed the proposal and proposed that the representatives of the clubs that favoured it should go ahead and organise it. He provided advice and wished them well but did not take part as he was opposed to violence.

About 200 people walked from the outskirts of Sheffield on to the moors at Bar Dyke and then followed The Duke of Norfolk's Road to the escarpment overlooking Abbey Brook, where about 100 permanent and temporary gamekeepers, armed with pick shafts, were gathered down in the valley below, expecting the ramblers to come from the opposite direction. With them were about half-a-dozen police who were determined to keep the occasion low-key.

After a 2-mile uphill walk the gamekeepers engaged in a brief scuffle with the ramblers, who having made their point sat down and ate their sandwiches before returning to Bar Dyke. The gamekeepers were furious with the police who declined to make any arrests, but the wisdom of this strategy ensured that the event was relatively peaceful and therefore starved of publicity. A smaller attempt at trespassing along Stanage Edge on 16 October was stopped by foot police with Alsatian dogs and mounted police, and a planned trespass along Froggatt Edge never materialised. According to Stephen Morton, it 'died from apathy'. Winter set in and nothing more was heard about mass trespassing. Nor had any gains been made by the access movement.

The continued struggle for access

In 1924 the growth of the outdoors movement and concern over the spread of housing into the countryside led to the formation of the Sheffield Association for the Protection of Local Scenery, with Ethel Gallimore, the future Mrs Ethel Haythornthwaite, as secretary. Three years later this association accepted an invitation from the newly created Council for the Preservation of Rural England (now the Campaign to Protect Rural England) to represent them in the Peak District. In the 1930s Ethel and

Gerald Haythornthwaite led the campaign for the designation of National Parks in Britain. Another prominent Sheffielder was Alderman J.G. Graves (1866–1945), a great public benefactor who employed 3,000 people in one of Britain's first mail order businesses. A Conservative councillor and former Lord Mayor, he appears on at least one photograph on the moors with the Sheffield Clarion Ramblers. He purchased and then presented to the City of Sheffield the Graves Art Gallery, Graves Park, Concord Park, Ecclesall Woods, Tinsley playing fields, the 448 acres of Blackamoor and land for the popular 10-mile Round Walk, and he made other purchases in the Peak District for public enjoyment.

In 1935 The National Council of Ramblers' Federations changed its cumbersome name to The Ramblers' Association on a motion proposed and seconded by two prominent members of the Sheffield Clarion Ramblers, Stephen Morton and Phil Barnes. In the first year of its life, The Ramblers' Association had almost 1,200 individual members and over 300 affiliated rambling clubs, though the Manchester Federation did not join until 1939. It was the RA that continued the access campaign once most of the mass trespassers had lost interest. Their objective was to obtain an Act of Parliament that would allow 'the right to roam' over mountains and moorland.

In 1934 Phil Barnes, who had been involved in the Abbey Brook trespass, published a booklet, with Ward's enthusiastic endorsement, entitled *Tresspassers Will be Prosecuted*. He showed that the owners of the seventeen Peak District moors where access was refused comprised three dukes, one earl, two knights, two army officers, eight industrialists and one local authority. Barnes argued: 'No true hill lover wants to see more footpaths in the wild heart of the Peak each nicely labelled with trim signposts and bordered by notices telling one not to stray. What he does want is the simple right to wander where fancy moves him.'

Meanwhile, in 1933 Tom Stephenson (1893–1987) had become a journalist, writing about the countryside for the Labour-supporting newspaper *The Daily Herald*. He addressed the annual Winnats Pass rally the following year, then in 1935 he wrote about his inspired idea of a 'Pennine Way', stretching from Edale and Kinder Scout to Scotland. From 1948 Stephenson was the Secretary of The Ramblers' Association, although the post did not become a full-time salaried position until 1952. He was a tireless campaigner for walkers' rights and he personally organised well-publicised treks in the Pennines for influential Labour MPs, lobbying their support.

The Access to Mountains Act (1939), introduced as a Private Members' Bill by Arthur Creech Jones, the Labour MP for Shipley, on behalf of the Ramblers' Association, proved a great disappointment for it was savaged by Conservative MPs, with numerous amendments and clauses that limited access and penalised trespassers. The lobbying on behalf of the Bill included an RA deputation to the Parliamentary Secretary, consisting of four prominent members: Bert Ward, Phil Barnes, Alfred J. Brown and C. E. M. Joad. The act was overtaken by the Second World War and the access campaign was put on hold, but during these years the Ramblers forged strong links with the Labour Party and acquired some well-placed and prominent supporters. It was a reflection of changed attitudes that John Dower's report on the new national parks (1945) proposed a legal right to roam over all uncultivated land in England and Wales.

The Second World War and its aftermath

During the Second World War many of the local moors were used for military training, just as they had been during the First World War, when a camp was established and practice trenches were dug near Redmires. The Eastern Moors were used by both the Airborne Division and the Home Guard, and rock outcrops, guide stoops and bridges were used for target practice and so have many scars from bullets and mortar bombs. Some sections of 'Dad's Army' even buried ancient guide stoops so that they would not provide directions for enemy parachutists. Between 1941 and 1945 British and Canadian troops used the Burbage Valley, American troops trained on Morridge, and British and Polish troops occupied Midhope Moors. In all these areas unexploded munitions remain buried in the peat. Slit trenches and gun platforms can still be found on some moors and searchlight battery earthworks survive in Edale and at Matlock. More spectacularly, a decoy to attract bombers was built on Houndkirk Moor to deflect raids on Sheffield. An elaborate arrangement of lights and fires contained in baskets and trenches was designed to replicate Sheffield's railway marshalling yards as seen from the air by night. Other decoys on Stanage, Eaglestone Flat and elsewhere were designed by film companies to imitate aircraft, buildings and sheds, but these devices were installed too late to deflect the destructive blitz attack on Sheffield in December 1940.

The election of a Labour government in 1945 brought a new impetus to the campaign by the Ramblers' Association, the CPRE and other bodies

The remains of a brick structure that was built as a target for military manoeuvres during the Second World War can be seen on Midhope Moors. Penistone parish is seen in the distance.

for the implementation of Dower's recommendations, which although somewhat watered down, culminated in the National Parks and Access to the Countryside Act (1949). Ten national parks were created in the upland parts of Britain, starting with the Peak National Park in 1951. A map was drawn to enclose 555 square miles within the park but to exclude large, built-up areas and industrial sites, especially around the Buxton quarries. The importance of the Hope cement works as the largest single employer in the Peak District was recognised, but otherwise severe restrictions were placed on large-scale industries and ribbon development was brought under control. The Act also charged highway authorities with the duty of preparing a definitive map of all routes that were considered to be public paths, and members of the Ramblers' Association responded enthusiastically by submitting evidence for thousands of claims. As a result, several agreements for public access were made at this time.

In 1954 the eleventh Duke of Devonshire allowed the public to roam over his part of Kinder Scout and three years later he granted the same right over Bleaklow, then in 1958 an agreement was reached on access across the remaining part of the Kinder plateau after the Peak Park Planning Board had threatened to issue orders on fifteen owners. Following ongoing pressure from the Ramblers Association, the Pennine Way Association,

The sixtieth anniversary of the creation of the Peak District National Park is celebrated at the dressing of the Eyam Townhead Well in the summer of 2011.

and other walkers' groups, the Pennine Way was designated as Britain's first official long distance footpath in 1951 and was finally opened on 24 April 1965, thirty years after Tom Stephenson's original article. It was soon followed by other trails, many of which were based on routes that were proposed and surveyed in detail by members of the Ramblers' Association. Important as these concessions were, they did not provide outright victory for the outdoors movement. The water companies, concerned about possible pollution of their reservoirs, sometimes issued permits to ramblers, but other landowners continued to refuse access.

The Ramblers' Association grew in strength during the 1960s and 1970s and many benefits for walkers were secured. For example, the RA persuaded the Ordnance Survey to depict on its popular maps the footpaths that were now marked on the new definitive maps of each local authority. For the first time ramblers were armed with information that showed precisely where they had a right to walk in the countryside. Further parliamentary lobbying led to the Countryside Act (1968), which insisted that county councils should signpost footpaths. But the battle for access was by no means won and the struggle continued for another generation. It was not until the end of the twentieth century, sixty-eight years after the mass trespass, that the Countryside and Rights of Way Act, passed by another Labour government, granted everyone the right to roam in open countryside, marked on Ordnance Survey maps as 'Access land'. England and Wales now have a total of 101,416 miles of public footpaths, 21,450 miles of public bridleways, 4,590 miles of roads used as public paths and 2,267 miles of byways open to all traffic – a density of 2.2 miles of public paths per square mile of land that is unparalleled anywhere else in the world.

Bert Ward died long before the battle was won and his influence declined as he grew old. A reward for his achievements came on 8 April 1945 when the Sheffield and District Federation of Ramblers' Associations presented him with the deeds to the 54½ acres of Ward's Piece on the summit of Lose Hill, across the Edale valley from Kinder Scout, which he immediately handed over to The National Trust. On 6 July 1957, shortly before he died, he was presented with the honorary degree of MA by the University of Sheffield, when the Public Orator said: 'No man could have worked more tirelessly for the preservation and accessibility of our countryside heritage and especially of the incomparable Peakland. No man, in the last half century, could have done more, by precept and example, to foster the true spirit of rambling.'

Finally, on 29 September 2009 Ward's Croft was opened as a garden at the educational resource, The Moorland Discovery Centre at Longshaw, by Linda Raby, Ward's granddaughter.

In the 1960s and 1970s left-wing intellectual and political interest in the historical struggles of the working classes, starting with the writings of E. P. Thompson and leading to confrontational politics, stimulated the growth of the legend of the mass trespass in which direct action by working-class groups (preferably those inspired by Marxism) was regarded as the triumphant way forward. At the same time, 'The Manchester Rambler' became a great favourite in the folk song revival. But Ewan MacColl's energies were concentrated on theatre and folk song and little more was heard of Benny Rothman in the campaign for access before 1982, when he was invited to join the 50th anniversary commemorations organised by The Ramblers' Association, whose new generation of officers seemed to be unaware that their organisation had once bitterly opposed him. The truth had been forgotten and, thanks to the great publicity it received at the time, the legend took over. So much so, that nowadays it is common to read on websites that The Ramblers' Association was founded in 1935 as a result of the mass trespass.

In fact, on 1 January of that year it merely changed its name from the National Council of Ramblers' Federations, which, as we have seen, had been founded at Longshaw in 1931. Yet in the 1980s David Beskine, the RA's access campaigner, was pleased to use this charismatic figure from the past. 'You can always rely on Benny for a bus-load of demonstrators,' he said. Rothman was encouraged to publish his account of the trespass for the fiftieth anniversary and to use his talents as a speaker at rallies and on radio and television.

The mass trespass certainly played an important part in publicising the struggle for access, but the fiftieth anniversary celebrations elevated it to the status of media icon.

Tom Stephenson's opinion of the 'spate of press publicity' was that much of it was 'misinformed and contrary to authentic available records'. Subsequent anniversaries have re-enforced the legend as a slick and simple, but inaccurate explanation of how the right to roam was won.

Chapter 8

Conclusion: Present Times

The farms on the edges of the moors have remained small, though many farmhouses were abandoned in the second half of the twentieth century or were converted into rural homes for commuters. The wartime returns to the Ministry of Agriculture and Fisheries early in 1942 showed that most farmers kept a herd of dairy shorthorns and a few other animals and poultry, but they had only a few acres of cereals and vegetables. A typical return was that of E.V. and A. Goldthorpe, corn millers of Bullhouse Mill, to the west of Penistone, whose crops were listed as 4½ acres of oats, 2½ acres of mixed corn with wheat, 1½ acres of potatoes, 1 acre of turnips and swedes for fodder, 2 acres of clover, sainfoin and temporary grasses for mowing this season, 15 acres of permanent grass for mowing, and 29½ acres of rough grazing: a total of 56 acres.

Their livestock comprised a mare, a gelding, a bull, two cows in milk, a cow in calf, five heifers in calf, twelve stirks or calves, two pigs and ten piglets, thirty-five fowls, forty-five chickens and nine ducks. Farm prices were guaranteed by the Agriculture Act (1947) and later European Union subsidies, which shifted the emphasis from dairying to the rearing of cattle and sheep, as the horse-and-cart and hand-tools era gradually gave way to tractors and machines. Yet most farms stayed small- or medium-sized and it remained common for men to combine the farming of a few acres with employment elsewhere. Some worked in the local drift mines until the seams of coal and gannister became exhausted in the 1950s and 1960s. Others found jobs with the local council, maintaining parks or trimming hedges and grass for the highways department, or in nearby quarries, mills and steel works.

Life in the Pennine farmsteads and hamlets did not alter much until electricity, gas and flushed toilets were installed. The worst time came during the winter months of January–March 1947, during the years of austerity after a long war and in the midst of a fuel crisis. Snow fell heavily and it was bitterly cold for weeks. By February many people had to dig themselves out of their houses through drifts 4 feet deep, while high winds drifted the snow on the moors to a depth of 6 to 8 feet. Flocks of sheep perished under the snow and people had to walk miles to railway goods stations to bring back coal on their sledges. It was not just a matter of keeping warm. Families were dependent on coal for fuel to do their cooking.

A typical moorland farmhouse or cottage had a Yorkshire range cast in iron and kept clean and bright by the arduous process of black leading. Each morning the ashes were emptied from the grate and a fire of newspapers, sticks and coal was set alight. A kettle of water was boiled directly

Curlews return each spring to nest on the moors. This characteristically simple nest was found on Leash Fen.

on the fire and pots and pans were hung from bars or stacked on the shelf below the mantelpiece. At one side of the fireplace a boiler contained a couple of gallons of water, on the other an oven was heated by the fire. All the cooking was done over the fire or in the oven, for only cold water could be obtained from the taps.

On Mondays a fire was lit under the set pot or copper in the corner beyond the oven, to provide hot water for the weekly clothes wash. On wet or cold days the washing had to be dried indoors on a wooden frame over the fire, where the smoothing iron was heated. Friday was bath night in a tin bath in front of the fire. Lighting was provided by paraffin lamps and candles. Home-made pegged rugs covered some of the stone flags. Mice and large beetles known as blackclocks scuttled across the hearth when it was dark. And the toilet was an earth closet across the farmyard.

In the last few decades these Pennine farmhouses have been modernised and made far more comfortable, sometimes by long-established farming families but often by incomers who do not derive their living from the land. The Peak District National Park Authority has restricted the sprawl of housing that had threatened to spoil the beauty of the countryside and insists on appropriate styles and materials when old farmhouses, cottages and outbuildings are renovated and turned into desirable rural dwellings. Men working for the Peak Park and the National Trust have skillfully restored long stretches of the drystone walls that give the Peak District so much of its distinctive character. The landscape has also been improved by individual initiatives, notably the plantation at Rosewood Farm, near Holmfirth, by George Bamforth, a poultry farmer who transformed 180 acres of bleak, wind-swept moorland 800 feet above sea level, by a life-long passion for planting sycamores and other trees. The countryside on the edges of the Pennines looks far more prosperous and well-tended now than it did a couple of generations ago.

The Peak District National Park Authority directly owns around five per cent of the park. Other major landowners include water companies and The National Trust, which established its High Peak estate in the 1950s when large stretches of moorland were transferred from the Dukes of Devonshire and Norfolk in lieu of death duties. In 1955 the 5,685 acres of Marsden Moor were presented to The National Trust by the Radcliffe family for the same reason, then in 1982 the Trust bought over 3,000 acres around Hayfield, which included Kinder Scout, the Downfall and two farms. The National Trust now owns twelve per cent of the Peak District National Park.

Edale from Hollins Cross. Burial parties on the old route from Edale to the parish church at Castleton, before the village got its own church in Victorian times, used to stop for prayers at Hollins Cross on the ridge dividing the two valleys. Edale is now the starting point for the long-distance Pennine Way that heads north along the Pennines.

The Peak Park Authority has to balance the recreational desires of an estimated 20 million people living within an hour's drive with the needs of the 38,000 residents. In the 1980s the Authority launched a rural development scheme to encourage tourism and establish small businesses. Tourism is estimated to provide 500 full-time jobs, 350 part-time jobs and 100 seasonal jobs within the Peak Park, which of course includes large parts of the White Peak and several stately homes as well as the gritstone moors. It is the major source of employment for Park residents (twenty-four per cent), followed by manufacturing industries (nineteen per cent), and quarrying and agriculture (another twelve per cent each).

Holiday homes, visitor and educational centres, walking and cycling trails, and special events laid on by the National Trust and other bodies help to cater for this trade. The greatest problem is caused by the amount of traffic that brings in tourists or services local industries, especially the limestone quarries. In an effort to reduce congestion and increase the enjoyment of the countryside, Cycle England began to invest £1.25 million over two years from 2009 to build and improve cycle routes within the National Park. One of the wildest areas left in the Peak District is the Alport Valley, which has no vehicular access to its hamlet.

The conifers that were planted in the 1930s by the Forestry Commission on moorland valley sides now present a problem as they cannot be extracted without a great deal of damage to the environment. Even those that are felled are of little value and are being replaced by deciduous trees with more aesthetic appeal. Several moors have been designated as Sites of Special Scientific Interest or as Environmentally Sensitive Areas, for which the owners receive payment, and in 2009 Kinder Scout was formally designated a National Nature reserve.

The National Trust and the Peak National Park Authority are committed to traditional management systems and to the regeneration of moors that have been badly affected by overgrazing, atmospheric pollution and uncontrolled fires. The Trust has introduced effective fire-fighting methods, rebuilt derelict walls, constructed effective boundary fences, rounded up stray sheep that should not have been there and applied light dressings of fertiliser and limestone dust to promote indigenous seeds to germinate. The results have been dramatic. The number of walkers and mountain bikers on the more popular paths in the Peak District, especially the Pennine Way, has brought serious erosion problems, particularly on the fragile peat moorlands of the Dark Peak. Measures taken to stop the damage have included the

The National Trust and the Peak National Park Authority have used lorries and helicopters to import flagstones from redundant Lancashire cotton mills in order to prevent footpath erosion. These paths have a pleasing resemblance to the causeys of the packhorse era. This view shows stones being laid on the climb from Jacob's Ladder up to the south-western edge of Kinder Scout.

diversion of the official route of the Pennine Way out of Edale, which now goes up Jacob's Ladder rather than following Grindsbrook, and the provision of firm surfaces over the peat bogs by laying down flagstones from disused cotton mills in Lancashire that have been transported by lorry and helicopter.

In the twentieth century Kinder Scout became one of the most damaged moorland districts in Britain, because of catastrophic wildfires, air pollution from the neighbouring industrial cities and a long history of overgrazing. Now considerable efforts are being made to restore its health. In 2002 the Heritage Lottery Fund provided the initial funding for the moors for the Future Partnership, which is based in Edale. The Peak District National Park Authority, Natural England, three water companies, the RSPB, The National Trust and Derbyshire County Council then joined forces to provide longer term funding. In 2009 the partnership secured £5.5 million from the EU Life+ Fund in order to launch a five-year scheme to reduce flood-risks and improve water supplies. This project is paying special attention to sphagnum moss, 'the most important peat forming plant and the glue that holds the whole blanket bog community together'. As sphagnum leaves are able to hold many times their weight in water, they prevent the bogs below from drying out and so help to provide a habitat for other plants and wildlife and to protect the peat from erosion.

Blanket bogs trap vast quantities of rainfall on the moors and release it slowly to the farmland, rivers and reservoirs below. They also provide food and habitats for migrating and resident birds, insects and mammals and capture the carbon dioxide that would otherwise enter the atmosphere with a greenhouse effect. Then in the spring of 2010 an ambitious programme of regenerating 2,000 acres attracted further funding. Sphagnum moss seeds and fertilisers were distributed across the moors by helicopter and other restoration work, including the blocking of gullies, re-seeding with heather, cottongrass, bilberry, crowberry and cloudberry, and the control of bracken, was begun by wardens and volunteers.

The hand-planting of 800,000 cottongrass plants over a period of five years is now well-advanced. In 2011 a stock exclusion fence (with stiles for ramblers) was erected to tackle the long history of over-grazing. A huge area adjacent to the Pennine Way has been treated with lime, grass, sand, fertiliser and heather brash, and degraded peat bogs on Bleaklow and Kinder Scout are now full of vegetation. The birds that have returned include buzzards and ravens that have long been absent.

One of the greatest problems on the Peak District moors is the tremendous spread of bracken, which is no longer cut as litter for horses and cattle, nor as fuel or thatch, nor as a source of potash for the making of soap, glass or fertilisers. The problem is caused largely by the over-grazing of sheep, whose numbers trebled after the Second World War. Sheep prefer to graze the more palatable grasses, but when these are gone or die back in winter, they turn to heather. As a result, bracken encroaches upon and eventually suppresses the heather. European Community regulations prohibit the aerial spraying of herbicides such as Asulam where moors are close to drinking water (as they often are), so the control of bracken is an expensive, difficult and long-term task.

Recent experimental mowing in the Upper Derwent Valley – at Ox Hey, Cow Hey and Black Dyke – and a reduced number of sheep point the way forward. The effects of grazing by sheep have long been demonstrated by the landscape on both sides of a barbed wire fence at the top of Padley Wood, which was installed by the Botany Department of Sheffield University and

In modern times bracken has spread at the expense of heather over large stretches of moorland, such as in this scene below the Stanage escarpment. This is partly because bracken is no longer harvested, but largely because of over-grazing of heather by sheep. Experiments at controlling the spread are underway, but the aerial spraying of herbicides is banned because of the risk of contaminating the water.

The National Trust. One side consists of heather and grass, the other is full of trees. Silver birch is always the first to spread across moorland if it is allowed to. This is particularly evident above the Surprise View car park. The birch trees were not there forty years ago, but now the wind spreads a few more seeds further east each season.

Looking across from Longshaw Lodge, we can see immediately how decisions about the management of the landscape have influenced the appearance of the moors. And looking at the spreading silver birch we get a sense of how some of the moors must have looked in prehistoric times.

Bibliography

Ainsworth, S., 'Prehistoric Settlement Remains on the Derbyshire Gritstone Moors', *Derbyshire Archaeological Journal*, cxxxi (2001), pp. 19–69

Ainsworth, S. and Barnatt, J., 'A Scarp-Edge Enclosure at Gardom's Edge, Derbyshire', *Derbyshire Archaeological Journal*, cxviii (1998), pp. 5–23

Ardron, P.A., 'Peat Cutting in Upland Britain with Special reference to the Peak District: Its Impact on Landscape, Archaeology and Ecology', unpublished PhD thesis, University of Sheffield (1999)

Barnatt, J., 'Neolithic and Bronze Age Radiocarbon Dates from the Peak District: a review', *Derbyshire Archaeological Journal*, cxv (1995), pp. 5–19

Barnatt, J., 'Taming the Land: Peak District Farming and Ritual in the Bronze Age', *Derbyshire Archaeological Journal*, cxix (1999), pp. 19–78

Barnatt, J., 'To Each Their Own: Later Prehistoric Farming Communities and their Monuments in the Peak', *Derbyshire Archaeological Journal*, cxx (2000), pp. 1–86

Barnatt, J. and Smith, K., *The Peak District: Landscapes Through Time*, 2nd edn (Bollington: Windgather, 2004)

Barnatt, J. and Williamson, T., *Chatsworth: A Landscape History* (Bollington: Windgather, 2005)

Barnatt, J. and Bannister, N., *The Archaeology of a Great Estate: Chatsworth and Beyond* (Oxford: Windgather, 2009)

Beedham, A., *Days of Sunshine and Rain: Rambling in the 1920s* (Sheffield: privately published, 2011)

Bevan, B., *The Upper Derwent: 10,000 Years in a Peak District Valley* (Stroud: Tempus, 2004)

Blanchard, I.S.W., *The Duchy of Lancaster's Estates in Derbyshire, 1485–1540* (Derbyshire Archaeological Society Record Series, 3, 1971)

Booth, P. H. W., (ed), *Accounts of the Manor and Hundred of Macclesfield, Cheshire, Michaelmas 1361 to Michaelmas 1362* (The Record Society of Lancashire and Cheshire, CXXXVIII, 2003)

Bowles, C.E.B., 'Concerning the Commons and Waste Lands in Various Townships in the High Peak', *Derbyshire Archaeological Journal*, xxiv (1902), pp. 32–41

Brighton, T., *The Discovery of the Peak District* (Chichester: Phillimore, 2004)

Brotherton, P. 'Celtic Place-Names and Archaeology in Derbyshire', *Derbyshire Archaeological Journal*, 125 (2005), pp. 100–37

Brown, R., *et al.*, *A General View of the Agriculture of the West Riding* (London, 1799)

Brumhead, D. and Weston, R., 'Seventeenth-Century Enclosures of the Commons and Wastes of Bowden Middlecale in the Royal Forest of Peak', *Derbyshire Archaeological Journal*, cxxi (2001), pp. 244–86

Camden, W., *Britannia* (London: 1588)

Cameron, K., *The Place-Names of Derbyshire*, 3 vols (Cambridge University Press, 1959)

Crook, D., 'The Forest between the Erewash and the Derwent, 1154 to 1225', *Derbyshire Archaeological Journal*, ciii (1990), pp. 98–106

Crook, D., 'The Development of Private Hunting Rights in Derbyshire, 1189–1258', *Derbyshire Archaeological Journal*, cxxi (2001), pp. 232–43

Crossley, D. and Kiernan, D., 'The Lead Smelting Mills of Derbyshire', *Derbyshire Archaeological Journal*, cxii (1992), pp. 6–47

Defoe, D., *A Tour through the Whole Island of Great Britain* (London: Everyman edn, 1962)

Doe, V.S. (ed.), *The Diary of James Clegg of Chapel en le Frith, 1708–55*, parts 1–3, Derbyshire Record Society, ii (1978), iii (1979) and v (1981)

Dransfield, J.N., *History of Penistone* (Penistone: Wood, 1906)

Edmonds, M. and Seaborne, T., *Prehistory in the Peak (Stroud: Tempus, 2001)*

Farey, J., *General View of the Agriculture and Minerals of Derbyshire*, 3 vols (London: Board of Agriculture, 1811–17)

Faull, M.L. and Moorhouse, S.A. (eds), *West Yorkshire: An Archaeological Survey to AD 1500*, 4 vols (Wakefield: West Yorkshire County Council, 1981)

Fowkes, D.V. and Porter, G.R. (eds), *William Senior's Survey of the Estates of the First and Second Earls of Devonshire, c. 1600–28*, Derbyshire Record Society, xiii (1998)

Garton, D., 'Buxton', *Current Archaeology*, 103 (1987), pp. 250–3

Greenslade, M.W. (ed), *A History of the County of Stafford, vii: Leek and the Moorlands* (Oxford University Press for the Institute of Historical Research, 1996)

Harris, B.E. (ed), *The Victoria County History of Cheshire*, II (Woodbridge: Boydell & Brewer, 1979)

Harrop, J. (ed), *Extent of the Lordship of Longdendale* (The Record Society of Lancashire and Cheshire, CXL, 2005)

Hey, D., 'The Dragon of Wantley: Rural Popular Culture and Local Legend', *Rural History*, 4, 1 (1993), pp. 23–40

Hey, D., 'The Distinctive Surnames of Staffordshire', *Staffordshire Studies*, 10 (1998), pp. 1–28

Hey, D., 'Yorkshire's Southern Boundary', *Northern History*, xxxvii (December 2000), pp. 31–48

Hey, D., *Packmen, Carriers and Packhorse Roads: Trade and Communications in North Derbyshire and South Yorkshire*, 2nd edn (Ashbourne: Landmark, 2001)

Hey, D., *Historic Hallamshire* (Ashbourne: Landmark, 2002)

Hey, D., *A History of Penistone and District* (Barnsley: Wharncliffe Books, 2002)

Hey, D., *Medieval South Yorkshire* (Ashbourne: Landmark, 2003)

Hey, D., 'Barlow: The Landscape History of a Peak District Township' in R.W. Hoyle (ed.), *People, Landscape and Alternative Agriculture: essays for Joan Thirsk* (British Agricultural History Society, 2004), pp. 1–29

Hey, D., *A History of Yorkshire: 'County of the Broad Acres'* (Lancaster: Carnegie, 2005)

Hey, D., 'The Grouse Moors of the Peak District', in P.S. Barnwell and M. Palmer (eds), *Post-Medieval Landscapes: Landscape History after Hoskins*, 3 (2007), pp. 68–79

Hey, D., *Derbyshire: A History* (Lancaster: Carnegie, 2008)

Hey, D., *A History of Sheffield*, 3rd edn (Lancaster: Carnegie, 2010)

Hey, D., 'Kinder Scout and the Legend of the Mass Trespass', *Agricultural History Review*, 59, pt II (2011), pp. 199–216

Hey, D., 'The Domestic Economy of the Seventeenth- and Eighteenth-Century Holmfirth Textile Industry', *Yorkshire Archaeological Journal*, 85 (2013), pp. 160–174.

Hey, D., 'Townfields, Royds and Shaws: The Medieval Landscape of a South Pennine Township', *Northern History* (2013), pp. 216–238.

Hey, D., 'The Medieval Origins of South Pennine Farms: the case of Westmondhalgh Bierlow, South Yorkshire', *Agricultural History Review*, (2014)

Hicks, S.P., 'The Impact of Man on the East Moor of Derbyshire from Mesolithic Times', *The Archaeological Journal*, 129 (1972), pp. 1–21

Hill, H., *Freedom to Roam: The Struggle for Access in Britain's Moors and Mountains* (Ashbourne: Moorland, 1980)

Howlett, D., *The Pioneer Ramblers, 1850–1950* (North Wales Area of the Ramblers' Association, 2002)

Hunter, J., *Hallamshire* (ed. Revd A. Gatty, London, 1869)

Jennings, L.J., *Rambles among the Hills in the Peak of Derbyshire and the South Downs* (London: Murray, 1880)

Kenworthy, J., *The Lure of Midhope-cum-Langsett* (Deepcar: privately published, 1927)

Kenworthy, J., *The Early History of Stocksbridge and District* (Deepcar: privately published, 1928)

Kerry, C., 'A History of Peak Forest', *Derbyshire Archaeological Journal*, xv (1893), pp. 67–98

Kerry, C. (ed), 'The Court Rolls of the Manor of Holmesfield, Co. Derby', *Derbyshire Archaeological Journal*, xx (1898), pp. 52–108

Morris, C. (ed), *The Illustrated Journeys of Celia Fiennes, c.1682–c.1712* (London: Macdonald, 1984)

Plot, R., *The Natural History of Staffordshire* (Oxford: 1686)

Postles, 'Rural Economy on the Grits and Sandstones of the South Yorkshire Pennines', *Northern History*, XV (1979), pp. 1–19

Purvis, J.S., (ed.), 'Select XVI Century Causes in Tithe', *Yorkshire Archaeological Society Record Series*, cxiv (1949), pp. 18–104

Rackham, O., *The Illustrated History Of The Countryside*. (London: Weidenfeld &

Nicolson, 2003)

Radley, J. and Mellors, P., 'A Mesolithic structure at Deepcar, Yorkshire, England, and the affinities of its associated flint industry', *Proceedings of the Prehistoric Society*, 30, pp. 1–24 (1964)

Redmonds, G., 'Turf Pits', *Old West Riding*, 7:1 (1987), pp. 13–14.

Redmonds, G., *Holmfirth: Place-Names and Settlement* (Lepton: privately published, 1994)

Roberts, A.F. and Leach, J.R., *The Coal Mines of Buxton* (Cromford: Scarthin Books, 1985)

Robinson, B., *Wall across the Valley: The Building of the Howden and Derwent Dams* (Cromford: Scarthin Books, 1993)

Ronksley, J.G. (ed.), *An Exact and Perfect Survey and View of the Manor of Sheffield with other lands. By John Harrison, 1637* (Hull Academic Press, 2009)

Rothman, B., *The 1932 Kinder Trespass* (Timperley: Willow, 1982)

Ryder, P.F., *Timber-Framed Buildings in South Yorkshire* (South Yorkshire County Council County Archaeology Monograph no. 1, no date)

Shoard, M., *A Right to Roam* (Oxford University Press, 1999)

Sissons, D. (ed), *The Best of the Sheffield Clarion Ramblers' Handbooks: 'Ward's Piece'* (Tiverton: Halsgrove, 2002)

Smith, A.H., *The Place-Names of the West Riding of Yorkshire*, 7 vols (Cambridge University Press, 1961–62)

Smith, H., *The Guide Stoops of the Dark Peak* (privately published, 1999)

Spencer-Stanhope, Sir W., 'Grouse driving at Dunford Bridge', *Country Life*, 27 August 1904, pp. 318–19.

Stephenson, T., *Forbidden Land: The Struggle for Access to Mountain and Moorland* (Manchester University Press, 1989)

Taylor, H., *A Claim on the Countryside: a History of the British Outdoor Movement* (Keele University Press, 1997)

Tebbutt, M., 'Gendering an upland landscape: masculinity and place identity in the Peak District, 1880s-1920s', in I. D. Whyte and A. J. L. Winchester (eds), *Society, Landscape and Environment in Upland Britain* (Society for Landscape Studies supplementary series 2, 2004), pp. 141–62

Thomas, A.H., 'Some Hallamshire Rolls of the Fifteenth Century', *Transactions of the Hunter Archaeological Society*, II, 1 (1920), pp. 65–79; II, 2 (1921), pp. 147–158

Tonkinson, M., *Macclesfield in the Later Fourteenth Century. Communities of Town and Forest* (Chetham Society, third series, xlii, 1999)

Turbutt, G., *A History of Derbyshire*, 4 vols (Cardiff: Merton Priory Press, 1999)

Winchester, A.J.L., *The Harvest of the Hills: Rural Life in Northern England and the Scottish Borders, 1400–1700* (Edinburgh University Press, 2000)

Index

Place-Name Index

Surnames Index

Discover Your History
Ancestors • Heritage • Memories

Each issue of *Discover Your History* presents special features and regular articles on a huge variety of topics about our social history and heritage – such as our ancestors, childhood memories, military history, British culinary traditions, transport history, our rural and industrial past, health, houses, fashions, pastimes and leisure ... and much more.

Historic pictures show how we and our ancestors have lived and the changing shape of our towns, villages and landscape in Britain and beyond.

Special tips and links help you discover more about researching family and local history. Spotlights on fascinating museums, history blogs and history societies also offer plenty of scope to become more involved.

Keep up to date with news and events that celebrate our history, and reviews of the latest books and media releases.

Discover Your History presents aspects of the past partly through the eyes and voices of those who were there.

FREE BOOK WHEN YOU SUBSCRIBE TO *Discover Your History*

UK only

Discover Your History is in all good newsagents and also available on subscription for six or twelve issues. For more details on how to take out a subscription and how to choose your free book, call 01778 392013 or visit **www.discoveryourhistory.net**